RAIL CENTRES:
EXETER

RAIL CENTRES:
EXETER

COLIN G. MAGGS

Nottingham

Booklaw Publications

First published 1985
by Ian Allan Ltd

©Ian Allan Ltd 1985

This edition published 2004 by
Booklaw Publications
382, Carlton Hill, Nottingham NG4 1JA

ISBN 1-901945-15-4

Printed by The Amadeus Press
Cleckheaton, West Yorkshire

Acknowledgements
Grateful acknowledgement for assistance is due to: M. H. Cobb; H. M. Davies, Cadbury Schweppes; M. E. J. Deane; A. Ellett; J. Heaton, BR Area Manager; R. A. Lumber; J. W. P. Rowledge; D. R. Steggles; P. K. Tunks; G. A. Walton, Western Fuels Ltd; M. White; C. W. Wood.
  A. J. C. Hill and E. S. Youldon have special thanks for checking the manuscript.

Contents

Outline History

The Romans founded Exeter about the year AD 50 calling it Isca Dumnoniorum as the people of Devon and Cornwall were known as Dumnonii and the river, the Isca. It was a frontier town on the edge of Roman territory as this race did not penetrate into the Celtic west. Isca became the Saxon Exa and the town Exancaster, eventually being shortened to the name we use today. The site of Exeter was chosen because it was at the head of the navigable waters of the River Exe and situated in a gap between Exmoor to the north and Dartmoor to the south west. At the beginning of the third century Exeter was fortified by a massive stone wall enclosing about 100 acres. In 876 Danish marauders captured it, King Alfred driving them out three years later. In 1003 the Danes again invaded and plundered the city, razed the walls and killed most of the population. In 1050 the rebuilt Saxon church became the seat of a bishop and later a new cathedral was constructed. Following the Norman Conquest, Exeter became the West's centre of resistance against William. Soon after 1200 the city had a mayor and about 35 years later the Exe was bridged.

From the tenth to the eighteenth century Exeter was a port of importance, at times ranking as high as third or fourth in the country, the city fitting out and manning three ships for the fight against the Spanish Armada. It was probably during the reign of Edward I (1272-1307) that Isabella de Fortibus, Countess of Devon, built a weir across the Exe, (still called Countess Wear), about three miles below the city bridge, barring access to Exeter by shipping. Following some 250 years of litigation the case was resolved in 1539 in favour of the citizens, but the river was found to be no longer navigable. To obviate this, in 1563 Exeter commissioned John Trew of Glamorganshire to cut a canal alongside the river, this being the first in Britain since Roman times. Three feet deep and 16ft wide, it was opened in 1566 accepting vessels up to 16tons which made transhipment with ocean-going craft lying in the estuary. In 1676 the canal was thoroughly dredged and extended half a mile towards Topsham to avoid a mile of difficult river, while in 1701 it was straightened and enlarged to 10ft deep and 50ft wide in order to accommodate coasting vessels and small deep-sea craft to about 150tons burden. Improvements completed in 1832 enabled the canal to take vessels of 14ft draught and 400tons. In 1843 two ships arrived weekly from London and there was both a coastal and foreign trade.

Devon Notes & Queries, Volume 6, gives a description of the Exeter Basin before the coming of the railway. 'I have seen from 20 to 30 vessels, two or three deep, lying there, and the ground covered with various goods and packages ... At this time the import of coals was immense, the surrounding towns and villages being supplied by the merchants. There were two trading companies for merchandise having about six vessels each, the tonnage from 120 to 180, sailing to and from London weekly, weather permitting. I have known goods delivered from London within the week, also some delayed more than a month.'

In June 1848 the *Malcolm Browne* started a weekly steamship service between Exeter Basin and London carrying goods and passengers in competition with the railway.

The first passenger stage coach service between Exeter and London began in 1658 and took four days to cover the 196 miles, while a stage coach from Exeter to Bristol and Bath began in 1727 and took three days to Bath. By 1764 improvement in road surfaces allowed the Exeter to London time to be reduced to two days, though the thrice weekly 'fly wagon' from the Mermaid, Exeter to London took 4½ days. By 1784 the time taken by the coach had been reduced to 32hr and in 1797 the Mail left London at 8pm, arrived Bath 10am and Exeter 10.40pm, a total of 26hr 40min for the journey making an average speed of about 7¼mile/hr. By 1828 the Devonport Mail reached Exeter from London in 19½hr and in 1835 16½hr. *Woolmer's Exeter & Plymouth Gazette* of 15 September 1838 said that the opening of the Southampton Railway to Antley Row, (actually Hartley Row, 38 miles from Nine Elms, opened 24 September 1838), would

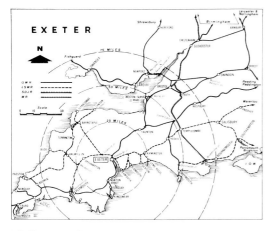

1. Rail routes to Exeter

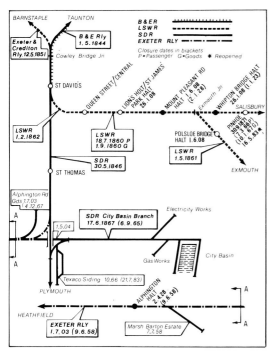

2. Diagrammatic representation of the railway history of Exeter

allow the *Defiance* and other coaches to be carried that distance in 1¾hr allowing the London to Exeter journey to be made 3hr faster. Exeter was an important coach centre with service to Plymouth, Liverpool, Manchester, Birmingham, Southampton and Portsmouth, local services running to Exmouth, Sidmouth, Dawlish, Teignmouth and Bideford.

Continuing with the history of Exeter, in 1911 the City Council endeavoured to purchase land to the north of Whipton Bridge Halt for use as an airfield,

but the project proved abortive. In November 1934 the Ministry of Air held a public inquiry into a proposal to serve a compulsory purchase order on land at Clyst Honiton, approval was given and the airport officially opened on 30 July 1938. It actually opened in 1937, Railway Air Services operating flights to Plymouth and Cardiff, while in 1939, Great Western & Southern Airlines began a daily service to Bristol-Exeter-Plymouth-Land's End-Scillies. In 1942 the city was the victim of a Baedeker raid; 1955 saw Exeter University awarding its own degrees and since WW2, three industrial estates have been established at Marsh Barton, Pinhoe and Sowton. Exeter is still an administrative capital of South West England and has the largest hinterland west of Bristol.

For the purposes of this book, Exeter can be defined as stretching on the GWR from Cowley Bridge Junction to the City Basin and Alphington Halt, and on the LSWR to Pinhoe and Polsloe Bridge Halt.

Population

1801	1851	1901	1931	1961	1981
17,398	32,823	47,185	66,029	95,598	100,500

1825 brought two railway schemes involving the city, the 'Bristol-Taunton-Exeter Rail Road', with a branch to Tiverton; and the 'Grand Western Rail Road' from London to Falmouth with a branch to Taunton and Bridgwater. Plans for these proved abortive, as did those for the Exeter & Crediton Railway for which an Act had been obtained in 1832 to run from the City Basin.

The Great Western Railway Act received Royal Assent in August 1835 and a month later Bristol merchants issued a prospectus for an extension of the broad gauge to Exeter. The bill had an easy passage through Parliament and the B&E Act received Royal Assent on 19 May 1836 authorising a capital of £1.5 million and borrowing powers of £0.5million. The line was to run from a junction with the GWR at Temple Meads and terminate 'at or near the City of Exeter in certain Meadows situate on the South-western side of the new Basin and Wharfs', though in the event, the line ended at Red Cow, St David's. Twelve of the directors were Bristol men, two came from Exeter and one each from Bridgwater and Taunton. Surprisingly, none were on the Great Western board.

Because about a quarter of the original shareholders had bought shares for speculation and failed to pay the calls, shortage of finance

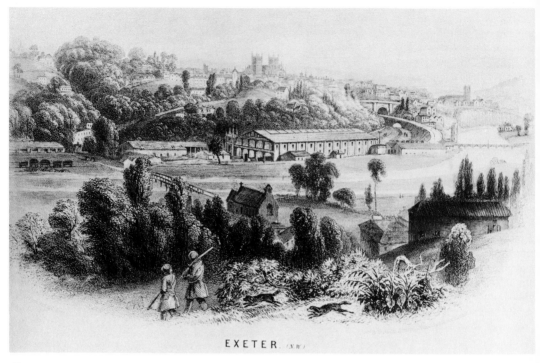

EXETER. (N.W.)

View of Exeter St David's from the north-west. Note the incline to St David's tunnel. *Devon Library Services*

caused the railway to be built in sections: that to Bridgwater opening on 14 June 1841; to Taunton 1 July 1842; to Beambridge 1 May 1843 – a temporary terminus where the turnpike road passed under the line about 1½ miles beyond Wellington; finally reaching Exeter on 1 May 1844.

Construction costs did not exceed the authorised sum, this being quite unusual in railway history. I. K. Brunel was the company's chief engineer, with William Gravatt his chief assistant and J. MacDonnell, resident engineer, works being carried out by numerous small contractors. Gravatt had worked with Marc and Isambard Brunel on the Thames Tunnel at Rotherhithe, but on the B&E proved to be unsatisfactory and let down his chief. Brunel censured him for 'a most unprofessional act' and on 23 July 1840 addressed him in a letter with the first two words of 'My dear Gravatt' deleted. A year later Gravatt was forced to resign.

The B&E was leased by the Great Western and the completion to Exeter meant that the GWR had a main line nearly 194 miles in length. The *Illustrated London News* reported that on 1 May 1844 'In Exeter all business was suspended and thousands and tens of thousands flocked in from the country;

and the streets, paraded by bands of music, were densely thronged with people in holiday attire'.

Sir Daniel Gooch, the GWR locomotive superintendent, gave a description of the opening run: 'We had a special train with a large party from London to go down to the opening. A great dinner was given in the Goods Shed at Exeter Station. I worked the train with the *Actaeon* engine, one of our 7 feet class, with six carriages. We left London at 7.30 am and arrived at Exeter at 12.30, having had some detention over the hour fixed'.

Adjoining the goods shed a marquee was erected to serve as a ladies' retiring room, also being used for an after dinner dance. 'On the return journey we left Exeter at 5.20pm and stopped at Paddington platform at 10. Sir Thomas Acland, who was with us, went at once to the House of Commons, and by 10.30 got up and told the House he had been in Exeter at 5.20. It was a very hard day's work for me, as, apart from driving the engine a distance of 387 miles, I had to be out early in the morning to see that all was right for our trip, and while at Exeter was busy with matters connected with the opening, so that my only chance of sitting down was for the hour we were at dinner. Next day my back ached so that I could hardly walk. Mr Brunel wrote me a very handsome letter, thanking me for what I had done, and all were very much pleased'.

A week after the opening of the B&E to Exeter, the completion of the Bristol & Gloucester Railway was the last link of a chain of rail communication from Exeter to Newcastle-on-Tyne, making Exeter, if not a railway centre, at least at the end of the line of communication. Between 1845 and 1848 various attempts were made at building a direct railway from Exeter to London, but all failed. The GWR's lease of the B&E ended on 1 May 1849 when the board decided it could work the line more economically itself. Coke ovens and carriage works were erected at Bridgwater and engine repairs temporarily provided for by minor additions to the existing depot at Exeter.

Although the mixed gauge was completed to Exeter from Taunton in November 1875, the station yard was still without the third rail and regular narrow gauge goods trains did not run to Exeter until 1 March 1876 and narrow gauge passenger trains not until July 1877. The B&E wanting to sell, wrote to the GWR in October 1875 stating that it must offer its line either to the GWR or to the Midland Railway. As the GWR did not wish for a repetition of the events six weeks previously when the Midland had snapped up the Somerset & Dorset Railway, the GWR lost no time in coming to a decision. On 11 October the B&E and GWR directors met at Paddington and agreed to a provisional lease of the B&E to the GWR from 1 January 1876 at a guaranteed rent of six per cent on its ordinary capital for the first seven years, and six and a half per cent subsequently. This was signed on 20 October and ratified by special meetings of both companies in December, the B&E being amalgamated with the GWR from 1 August 1876. As a dividend of six per cent had only twice been reached by the B&E, shareholders had secured a bargain.

J. B. Baron Collins writing in the *Railway Magazine* 1913 said 'Exeter people hoped that no lines would be constructed west of their city so that traffic should not pass without being much handled and passengers also, as far as their money was concerned. Bed and meals for a few hours at least, and then a coach journey to the regions beyond were thought more paying for Exeter than being what it has become, an excellent railway centre'. But the wishes of Exeter citizens were not to be. As soon as the B&E had reached the stage of Parliamentary authorisation, some enterprising inhabitants of Plymouth proposed an extension to their city and in the summer of 1836 Brunel surveyed a line via Torquay, but after the

locomotive had demonstrated its climbing abilities, adopted a more direct route. In 1843 the B&E, GWR and Bristol & Gloucester subscribed generously to the Plymouth, Devonport & Exeter Railway, its title soon amended to the simpler South Devon Railway. The bill had an easy passage through Parliament receiving Royal Assent on 4 July 1844 authorising a capital of £1.1million.

After the Act was passed, Messrs Samuda Bros & Clegg proposed that the directors adopted their patent atmospheric system. The matter was rightly referred to Brunel who reported favourably, the system was chosen and James Pearson appointed as engineer in charge. Briefly the atmospheric principle consisted of a 15in cast iron pipe in which a piston travelled being laid between the rails, stationary steam pumps exhausting air from it. To enable the piston to be connected to a special carriage to which a train could be coupled, the top of the pipe had a continuous slit closed by a leather flap. One edge of this longitudinal valve formed a hinge, while the other was sealed with grease to make it airtight, a roller behind the piston resealing this valve. The air in front of the piston being pumped out, atmospheric pressure behind the piston pushed forward it, the carriage and the train, leaving the valve closed and the pipe ready to be exhausted for the next train. The system had several advantages over locomotive haulage: collisions on a single line would be impossible; there would be no nuisance from coke dust and it was anticipated that speeds would be higher.

The contractors Samuda Bros & Clegg set to work and by February 1845 the viaduct of 62 stone arches at St Thomas was nearly completed. Because of a delay in the manufacture of the atmospheric machinery, the 15 miles of single line from the B&E station at St David's which the SDR leased for £1,300 per annum including all services, to Teignmouth were opened for passenger traffic on Whit Saturday 30 May 1846 using locomotives. The two 2-2-2 engines hired from the GWR for 1s 4d per ton/mile had been built by Haigh Foundry. Named *Snake* and *Viper* they were renamed *Exe* and *Teign* which was certainly better for SDR public relations. The first train left Exeter at 12.25pm and consisted of nine carriages hauled by *Teign*. At 1.27pm the train set off from Teignmouth on its return journey, arriving back at Exeter 38 minutes later giving an average speed of 23 miles/hr. On Sunday all the trains were filled, the *Exeter Flying Post* reporting 'the influx of persons either way was immense.' On Whit Monday a 21

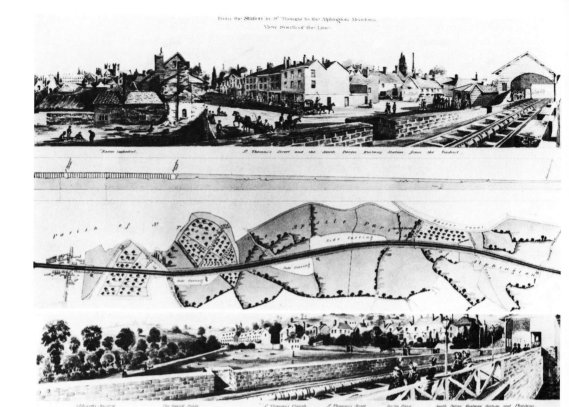

From the Station in S.t Thomas to the Alphington Meadows.
View South of the Line.

Above:

Views north and south at St Thomas station with the atmospheric pipe in position. *BR/OPC*

coach train carried 1,500 passengers.

Pump houses, each with a tall chimney disguised as an Italian campanile, were erected beside the line at intervals of about three miles, those in the Exeter district being east of the Exe Bridge at St David's and at Countess Wear. Each engine house contained two 41½hp engines able to work independently or coupled. In the spring of 1846 Messrs Boulton & Watt installed the engines at Exeter, Messrs Rennie supplying those for Countess Wear. On 25 February 1847 the first piston carriage was delivered and a test run made to Turf that very evening, the engineers apparently so excited at the prospect that they did not mind that most of the run would have been in the dark. The distance had to be of six miles because the intermediate engine house at Countess Wear was not operational. The resident engineer, P. J. Margery entered in his journal: 'Started at 6pm for Turf towing a locomotive behind. Went on very slowly to Turf there being a large quantity of water and dirt in the pipe'.

Delays in completing the pump engines meant that atmospheric trains did not reach Teignmouth until 16 August 1847 and from this date experimental atmospheric trains ran daily from Exeter, down trains leaving at 3pm and 6.30pm, up trains departing from Teignmouth at 10.45am and 4pm, none being available to members of the public. The scheduled journey time was 40min with intermediate stops at Starcross and Dawlish and speeds of up to 45mile/hr were reached. On 18 August a goods train of 11 wagons loaded to 120tons covered the 8¼ miles between Exeter and Starcross in 15min at an average speed of 33mile/hr. Early in September a daily goods was regularly worked atmospherically.

The line had opened with locomotive working from Teignmouth to Newton Abbot for passengers on 30 December 1846; and Exeter to Newton Abbot for goods on 1 May 1847; to Totnes 20 July and 6 December 1847 for passengers and goods respectively; Laira being reached on 5 May 1848 and Plymouth Millbay on 2 April 1849.

Meanwhile on 13 September 1847 two atmospheric trains began public working between Exeter and Teignmouth. 'Except when occasional mishaps caused delay, the new mode of traction was almost universally approved of. The motion of the train, relieved of the impulsive action of the locomotive, was singularly smooth and agreeable; and passengers were freed from the annoyance of coke dust and the sulphurous smell from the engine chimney'. Approaching a station the piston left the pipe, the train coasting in. 'An arrangement for starting the train rapidly from the station, without help of horses or locomotives, has been brought practically into operation. This consisted of a short auxiliary vacuum tube containing a piston which could be connected with the train by means of a tow-rope and thus draw it along till the piston of the piston carriage entered the main atmospheric tube. Some accidents at first occurred in using this apparatus, but its defects were after a time removed'. The highest speed attained by atmospheric traction was 68mile/hr with a train of 28ton and 35mile/hr with 100ton. Subsequently further trains were transferred from locomotive to atmospheric working. On 25 September the 9.50am from Exeter consisting of five coaches made an average speed of 60mile/hr between Countess Wear and Turf. The trip was described as virtually free from noise and so smooth that it was possible for the reporter to write with ease while travelling at 40-50mile/hr. An inspection of the guards' journals from September 1847 to January 1848 showed that of the atmospheric trains over that period, 790 were either on schedule or arrived early, against a debit of 94 late trains, 70 of these being only up to 5min late. Teignmouth to Newton Abbot was opened to atmospheric traction on 17 December and by 10 January 1848 the majority of trains from Exeter-Newton Abbot were atmospherically worked and on 23 February the changeover was complete.

However the system did not have the success anticipated, problems abounded: the leather valve did not make an airtight seal; the leather itself deteriorated; the pumping engines were inefficient and unreliable; the proposed telegraph between the pump houses had yet to be installed so fuel was wasted when pumps exhausted air on time for a train which was late. Atmospheric traction continued after a fashion for eight months and locomotive working resumed on Sunday 10 September 1848. £433,991 had been spent on what Devonians referred to as the 'Atmospheric Caper'

Below:
Mixed gauge at Cowley Bridge junction c1890. The line to Crediton diverges to the left, with the Taunton line on the right. *GWR*

and only about £80,000 of this was recovered by the sale of plant. The SDR was saddled with 40 miles of single line and a set of gradients that are a problem to this day.

On 18 December 1848 the SDR opened its branch to Torquay which helped increase Exeter's importance as a railway centre and led to the 'Torbay Express' of later years. The line was extended to Paignton on 2 August 1859 and to Kingswear on 16 August 1864. The SDR's single main line caused delay at holiday times and on 18 July 1850 some trains took as long as 6hr to travel from Plymouth to Exeter instead of 2¾hr. Doubling began in 1855, that from Exminster to St Thomas being finished in June 1861 and onwards to St David's in September the same year. Facing LSWR competition in the mid-1870s and yearly increasing charges for the maintenance and renewal of the permanent way, the directors agreed to amalgamation with the GWR, terms being £65 of Great Western ordinary stock, to be increased after seven years to £70, for each £100 of SDR ordinary stock. These terms were ratified at a special meeting on 17 December 1875. The agreement was that the SDR was to be worked by the GWR for 99 years commencing 1 February 1876, though in fact the arrangement was to last less than 18 months as the two companies merged under an Amalgamation Act of 22 July 1878, the SDR being dissolved on 1 August 1878.

The Exeter & Crediton Railway Act of 23 June 1832 gave powers for a line from the City Basin, but expired without any action being taken. The idea was resurrected in 1844, the broad gauge line

modified to join the B&E at Cowley Bridge. This Act received Royal Assent on 21 July 1845 and authorised a capital of £70,000, the following year the Taw Vale Extension Railway receiving powers for extending it to the North Devon capital of Barnstaple. The same year the Taw Vale was leased to the LSWR which aimed to control the E&C. It had been understood that the broad gauge E&C would be leased to the B&E, but E&C shareholders rejected this proposal. Thomas Brassey won the contract to build the E&C to the mixed gauge, but the complicated gauge question delayed opening. The original Taw Vale Railway from Fremington to Barnstaple was narrow gauge; the E&C mixed gauge and that of the Taw Vale Extension as yet unfixed. The matter was settled on 8 February 1848 when the Railway Commissioners ruled that the Taw Vale Extension should be laid to the broad gauge. The directors of the E&C informed the Commissioners that narrow gauge trains would start from Crediton and run to a temporary station at Cowley Bridge on 15 February 1848; however all was to no avail as the LSWR cancelled the E&C opening greatly to the annoyance of the proprietor of the Ship Hotel, Crediton who had laid in large stocks of champagne and bought an omnibus to connect with trains. The E&C was leased to the B&E and opened on 12 May 1851, the train of five coaches leaving Crediton at 1.0pm. Nevertheless the line remained unworked for another three years, the sole income being derived from the hay crop that was regularly gathered from the grass that grew on the unused railway. The Taw Vale Extension, which had been renamed the North Devon Railway, opened to Barnstaple and Fremington on 1 August 1854 and to Bideford on 2 November 1855. The LSWR leased the E&C from 1 February 1862 and amalgamated the Bideford Extension and the NDR on 1 January 1865, purchasing the E&C in 1879. Narrow gauge trains reached Bideford on 1 March

1863, though a daily broad gauge goods continued to run until 1877, while the B&E and GWR retained goods rights to Crediton until 1903, the daily train being broad gauge until 1892. The LSWR reached Plymouth via Cowley Bridge Junction, Coleford Junction and Lydford on 17 May 1876, the LSWR directors and officials together with the mayor of Exeter leaving Queen Street at 11.5am in a decorated special train. The opening of this line was important to Exeter as it meant that as well as being on the main route from Paddington to Penzance, it was on an alternative line to Plymouth, in fact apart from traffic using the Devon & Somerset Railway between Barnstaple and Taunton, all rail borne traffic from Devon and Cornwall had to pass through the city.

As the B&E approached Exeter from the North-east there was scope for building a line approaching from the east. As early as 1836, Francis Giles, engineer of the London & Southampton Railway, projected a route from Basingstoke through Salisbury and Honiton. The Salisbury & Yeovil Railway obtained its Act of Parliament in July 1848, not without difficulty, the GWR trying to get it built to the mixed gauge, even going so far as to offer to lay the extra line at its own expense, but Parliament turned down this offer. Financial difficulties arose the same year and the LSWR was unable to provide the promised £440,000, the project was shelved temporarily, but in 1854 the LSWR agreed to work and maintain the Salisbury & Yeovil Railway and a new Act was obtained as powers had lapsed. To lower the initial costs, although works were wide enough for double track, – the company had the foresight to see that it would develop into an important through route – only a single line was actually laid. In the meantime a cut-off had been opened between Andover and Salisbury shortening the distance to London.

The SYR was completed on 1 June 1860. The extension line from Yeovil onwards to Exeter Queen Street was owned by the LSWR and sanctioned by an Act of 21 July 1856. John Edward Errington was the engineer, with William Robert Galbraith as resident engineer, and James Taylor of Northernhay, Exeter, the contractor. Fortunately the 263yd-long Black Boy Tunnel at Exeter gave little trouble. The special train carrying directors left Waterloo at 8am on 18 July 1860, the 20 coaches being hauled by *Britannia*, *Montrose* and *Vulcan*. The first and last were 'Vesuvius' class 2-2-2s, while *Montrose* was of the 'Canute' class with the same wheel arrangement. They arrived at Exeter at 3pm. A holiday was granted in the city, the occasion alo being marked by a total eclipse of the sun in the afternoon. The *Western Times* reported: The shops were some shut and some open, flags were put out by some of the citizens, but the display was not general, nor was the feeling enthusiastic'. As rain seeped through the marquee canvas, toasts were offered to the directors. Public services began the following day, though goods traffic did not commence until 1 September. The line was doubled from Broad Clyst to Exeter on 11 April 1864.

The LSWR planned to connect with the B&E at St David's and the SDR at St Thomas, but the building of the latter spur was strongly opposed. On 3 July 1860 the LSWR obtained an Act for extending its line to St David's, to contribute towards the station's rebuilding and laying down narrow gauge to Cowley Bridge Junction and also over the Exeter & Crediton, North Devon Railway and Bideford Extension lines, thus forming a continuous narrow gauge from Waterloo to Bideford, a distance of 219½ miles. James Taylor carried out the £19,550

contract for extending to St David's down a gradient of 1 in 37 which included cutting the 184yd long St David's Tunnel. The line opened on 1 February 1862, the same date as the mixed gauge from St David's to Cowley Bridge Junction.

The opening of the LSWR affected B&E receipts, the LSWR route being 22 miles shorter to London, so the B&E had to reduce its fares by the same amount. The B&E chairman, J. W. Buller is reported to have said on 28 February 1862 that: 'However great might be the advantage offered by the broad gauge system which had been fully displayed during the past half year, they should reduce their fares by the same amount . . . Though the line had been open for more than six months, the shareholders and the public had not heard of that unseemly competition, which had existed among other competing railway companies (cheers); they had no scandal to complain of in any way (hear, hear). They had been engaged in an honourable and friendly rivalry, the object of both companies being not to take any traffic from each other, but to be rivals as to which should serve the public the best . . . he was happy to say that the public had shown preference for the old line (cheers)'.

To counter the Great Western's Castle Cary-Cogload Junction cut-off opened in 1906 which allowed that company to be more competitive for Plymouth traffic, the same year the LSWR planned a deviation line from Queen Street running west of the GWR line to just north of Cowley Bridge, the object being to avoid delays caused by having to cross on the level and use GWR metals. Lord Robertson as arbitrator decided that LSWR should not make the deviation as it would have contravened the Heads of Agreement of 21 October 1882. At a meeting with the GWR, Sir Charles Scotter, chairman of the LSWR, suggested delays might be avoided by shortening the block from Cowley Bridge Junction and the next GWR block eastwards, and by allowing two LSWR trains each way to run through St David's without stopping, but the GWR would not countenance this plan.

As early as 1825 plans were made for opening a railway from Exeter to Exmouth, but came to naught. In the 1840s the people of Exmouth found it very frustrating to see trains the other side of the river carrying tourists to Dawlish, Teignmouth, and Torquay, and coveted a share of this lucrative holiday traffic. During the Railway Mania two schemes were put forward: a broad gauge plan for a branch from either St David's station, or the SDR

at Countess Wear, across the river to Topsham and on to Exmouth; while a narrow gauge party proposed a scheme for a line following the east bank of the river from the Exeter City Gaol to Exmouth. The latter project was successful in Parliament, but was not proceeded with when the Exeter, Yeovil & Dorchester Railway scheme with which it was connected proved abortive. The failure to build the line rather embarrassed an enterprising Exmouth hotelier who had already named his premises the 'Railway & Commercial'.

In 1854 the proposal for a branch from Exminster on the SDR was again put forward and while being cross-examined about the scheme in the House of Commons Committee, its engineer was asked, 'Pray, Mr Brunel, did you ever know a Parliament sanction a bridge over a tidal river which bridge compelled vessels to lower their mast?' 'Yes,' replied the civil engineer, 'I rather think I do.' 'Have the goodness to tell me where it is?' 'Why, here, close to this House, and if you step to the window I will show it to you.' His cross-examiner dropped the subject without looking at Hungerford Bridge. The Exeter & Exmouth Railway bill received Royal Assent 2 July 1855. On 1 August 1857 the directors reported that they had arranged for the B&E and SDR to lease the line, but shareholders appointed a committee which rejected this action, preferring a connection with the LSWR. In September the LSWR resolved to make a branch from Exeter to Topsham, with the Exmouth Company continuing to Exmouth, the two companies sharing the cost of Topsham station. The Exmouth company was authorised by an Act of 28 June 1858 to carry out these modifications, the LSWR receiving powers on 12 July.

J. E. Errington was appointed engineer with W. R. Galbraith as resident engineer, bridges and stations being to the designs of Sir William Tite. James Taylor won the contract for the Exmouth section. On 1 May 1861 the first train consisting of 11 coaches and carrying about 150 passengers left Queen Street at 7.46am drawn by No 36 Comet, a 2-2-2 well tank, decorated with flags. Thirty minutes later it arrived at Exmouth.

The second train arrived with 500 passengers in 19 coaches behind two locomotives and the third, again piloted, consisted of 16 coaches. In the afternoon one of the guests at the banquet was the American George Francis Train of tramway fame who had opened two lines in London during the previous four weeks. A good speaker, he received applause and laughter when he remarked that 'but for the kind invitation I received from Mr Dutton (the Hon Ralph H. Dutton, LSWR director), you would have had today one Train the less'.

The LSWR worked the line and by Act of 5 July 1865 took over the local company on 1 January 1866. On 1 June 1908 doubling the track between Exmouth Junction and Topsham was completed at a cost of £16,000. Sixty years later it had been intended that it would be singled again as an economy measure during the currency of the 1967-8 timetable, but during this period the railway engineering department's resources were concentrated on singling the Wilton South to Pinhoe main line. This meant that it was neither financially or physically possible to encompass this small task. On the Exmouth branch trains continued to use each track and from 5 May 1969 the Working Timetable route map reverted to showing double line. This situation lasted until 1 May 1972 when the map indicated the section as single line in anticipation of it occurring during the currency of the 1972-3 timetable, the engineering and signalling departments actually singling the line between Saturday 3 February and Monday 5 February 1973.

Although not literally one of Exeter's railways, the Exe Valley line from Stoke Canon Junction, 3½ miles up the line from St David's, and running to Morebath Junction, was of significance to Exeter because trains terminated at St David's rather than Stoke Canon. This was because the original Stoke Canon station was sited on the up side of the branch junction, the first Stoke Canon station serving the Valley being opened on 1 July 1894 and enlarged in 1931. The Exe Valley Railway was authorised on 30 June 1874 to connect Tiverton with the B&E main line at Stoke Canon. The company had proposed an extension to a junction with the Norton Fitzwarren to Barnstaple branch, but in the event this was built by the Tiverton & North Devon Railway which opened on 1 August 1884. The powers of the Exe Valley Railway were taken over by the B&E in 1875, though by the time the contractor W. Moss of Stafford began work, the B&E had in turn been taken over by the GWR. W. B. Berry of Crediton built the stations. The line opened on 1 May 1885, the GWR running trains from St David's to Dulverton. The passenger service ceased on 7 October 1963 though grain traffic continued between Stoke Canon and Thorverton until this section succumbed on 30 November 1966.

On 4 July 1866 Newton Abbot and Moretonhampstead were linked by the broad gauge Moretonhampstead & South Devon Railway worked by the SDR. Investors saw scope for building a line from Heathfield on the Moretonhampstead line, up the Teign Valley to Chagford, midway throwing off a branch which would have tunnelled through the Haldon Hills to Exeter. After no less than nine Acts had been passed, the isolated narrow gauge project reached Ashton on 9 October 1882, goods trains continuing another 1¼ miles to Teign House, later known as Christow. The following year the Exeter, Teign Valley & Chagford Railway was authorised to construct a line from Exeter to Christow making an end on junction with the Teign Valley Railway and a 10-mile branch to Chagford. The GWR offered to work the line for 50% of gross receipts, allow rebates estimated to be worth £5,000 annually and the free use of St David's until the company earned £10,450 a year. The purpose of the line was to open up mineral deposits of ball clay, stone quarries, manganese, tin and copper mines and also provide an alternative to the coastal main line to Newton which sometimes suffered in storms. In due course, the 'Cornish Riviera' did use the branch, double headed by 4-4-0s of the 'Bulldog' or 'Flower' classes, 4-6-0s being too heavy. James & John Dickson won the contract for building the line and started work in 1896, the engineers being F. Bluett (the company's engineer) and J. H. Dickinson (the contractor's engineer), the latter founder of the Devon Basalt & Granite Co whose quarries were at Christow. Because investors failed to give it financial support, in 1897 the company had to obtain Parliamentary sanction to abandon the Chagford branch and at the same time the line's title was simplified to the Exeter Railway. It opened on 1 July 1903 connecting with the main line at Exeter Railway Junction, Exeter. Following a luncheon held in a marquee at the goods station in Alphington Road, the official train left St Thomas at 3.40pm and was welcomed at each station, guests having tea at Christow before returning. On 1 May 1904 a spur linked the Exeter Railway with the City Basin branch. Although leased and worked by the GWR, the Exeter Railway remained independent until 1923 when it became amalgamated with the GWR. Passenger services over the branch were withdrawn on 9 June 1958 and the section from Alphington Sidings to Christow closed completely. Although this alternative route to Newton was no longer available, for a few years until 6 May 1968 diversions could still be made via the former LSWR route from Exeter to Plymouth. To complete the story, Christow and Ashton were closed on 1 May 1961, Trusham following on 5 April 1965 and Chudleigh on 4 December 1967.

Development of Passenger Services

In May 1844 the opening service on the B&E consisted of seven trains daily each way. Although the line from London was splendidly straight and almost level, in January 1845 the fastest train on the line, the 'Night Mail', took 7hr 10min from London to Exeter giving an average speed including stops of 27 mile/hr. The poor speed of GWR trains was one of the reasons which led to the 'Five Kings' of the Gauge Commission at the Board of Trade reporting in January 1845 against the broad gauge, so the Great Western board resolved to make accelerations. On 10 March the 9.30am from Paddington arrived in Exeter 5hr later (39 mile/hr), in May 4½hr (43 mile/hr) and in December 1847 4hr 25min making it the fastest train in the world by a good margin, but in May 1849 the B&E added stops at Weston Junction and Tiverton Junction increasing the time to 4hr 40min. In 1849 the train was named the 'Flying Dutchman' after a horse which that year had won both the Derby and the St Leger. Probably with economy in mind these schedules came to an end in 1852 and from 1 January 1853 the best train took 5¼hr.

The 'Night Mail' which left Paddington at 8.55pm also carried passengers and being a heavy train with frequent stops was a poor timekeeper, particularly in winter. From 1 February 1855 Rowland Hill arranged for a London & Exeter Travelling Post Office, (the 'Special Mail'), consisting of two sorting carriages and a van hauled by a 'Fire Fly' class locomotive. This left Paddington at 8.46pm, reached Bristol at 12.30am where, combining with a passenger train which had left Paddington at 8.10pm, the TPO arrived at Exeter at 3.20am, an improvement of 45min over previous mail schedules. The up mail, known officially as the 'Special Mail' and among railwaymen as the 'Little Mail', left Exeter at 9.45pm and arrived at Paddington 4.19am.

The next improvement in service was brought about by LSWR competition in February 1862 when the noon express from Waterloo was accelerated to run the 171½ miles in 4¾hr, 25min faster than the B&E's best which had to cover a distance of 194 miles. The B&E directors quickly arranged a conference between Saunders, Gooch, Kelley and Graham for the Great Western, Dykes (traffic superintendent of the B&E) and Cockshott of the SDR which resulted in the 'Flying Dutchman's' return to the 4½hr schedule of 1845-49 and a new Exeter express was put on to cover the distance in the same time. In December 1865 the Great Western increased the time to Bristol by 8min, the B&E making up for its partner's deficiencies and speeding its own schedule so that the train still arrived in 4½hr, but when in June 1867 the GWR added another 10min, the B&E inserted stops at Bridgwater and Tiverton Junction increasing the time to 5hr 5min. Despite this slow down, 'Express Fares' continued to be charged, these being 5s (25p) over the ordinary fares of £1.15s (£1.75) first class and £1.5s (£1.25) third. The LSWR also eased its schedules to 4hr 58min down and 5hr 22min up allowing the GWR to just keep ahead and avoiding expensive competition. The 'Dutchman' normally left Paddington with seven six-wheel coaches; at Swindon one each for Weymouth and Cheltenham were detached, while at Newton the train was divided, two running to Torquay and three to Plymouth. To help overcome financial problems, in November 1867 the 'Dutchman' was withdrawn and not, despite B&E pressure, re-instated until May 1869 still on the 4¾hr schedule.

In 1871 the LSWR speeded its service to 4½hr, the GWR retaliating by scheduling the 'Dutchman' to reach Exeter in only 4¼hr (45.6 mile/hr), while in 1874 the 2.10pm from Waterloo, frequently referred to as the 'Beeswing', reached Exeter in 4¼hr (40.4 mile/hr). A large notice board at the top of the Queen Street station slope proclaimed to passers-by, including those foolhardy enough to go to St David's, that the LSWR was the shortest route to London by 21 miles and that it ran a fast express in 4¼hr. On 17 May 1876 the LSWR reached Plymouth and a new afternoon express was timetabled from Waterloo. By 1879 it had been accelerated to reach Exeter in 4hr (42.7 mile/hr) and carried third class passengers which GWR expresses disdained to accommodate. The GWR replied in 1879 with the 'Zulu', a new narrow gauge train which reached Exeter in 4hr 14min equalling the speed of the still extant broad gauge 'Dutchman', the latter not carrying passengers of all three classes until 1890. The influence of James Grierson the general manager caused a new broad gauge express called the 'Jubilee' to be put on in July 1887 taking 4hr 37min to Exeter. It was especially for third class passengers who had virtually nothing except a very slow train between 9am and 5pm, and therefore used rival services from Waterloo. In 1890 the 'Cornishman' cut the time to Exeter to 4hr 5min (47.5mile/hr). The final broad gauge run of the 'Dutchman' was on 20 May 1892. The opening of the narrow gauge Weston-super-Mare loop on 1 March 1884 had meant that from this date all stopping trains from Bristol to Exeter were required to run on the narrow gauge. The first regular GWR narrow gauge passenger trains to Exeter began in July 1877 when one ran from Taunton to Exeter; then to Bristol and back to Exeter, finally returning home to Taunton, a distance of 212 miles in 15hr. The last broad gauge train left Exeter at 4am on 21 May 1892 and arrived Swindon 9.45am. The eradication of the broad gauge allowed through coaches to be run from Torquay to Manchester, Liverpool and Leeds.

With the abolition of the compulsory 10min refreshment stop at Swindon, on 20 July 1896 the Newquay section of the 'Cornishman' consisting of five coaches ran non-stop to Exeter in 3¾hr (51.7mile/hr) this being easily the longest non-stop run in the world. The following year two trains ran non-stop in each direction daily performing this feat. In the summer of 1901 the 'Cornishman' was speeded to reach Exeter in 3hr 38min (53.4mile/hr). On 14 July 1903 4-4-0 No 3433 *City of Bath* hauled the Duke and Duchess of Cornwall on a non-stop

trip from London to Plymouth which passed Exeter 2hr 52½min after leaving Paddington (67.5mile/hr) and four days later the 'Cornishman' was scheduled to make the run to Exeter in 3½hr (55.4mile/hr). It was at this period that passengers and mail traffic from the railway-owned docks at Plymouth began to develop, GWR tenders plying between ocean liners anchored in the Sound and Millbay Pier and thus saving a day or more. This traffic lasted until World War 2, 80-90 liners calling each month and in the 1930s prestige 'Super Saloons' with 9ft 7in wide bodies were built for this traffic.

On 1 July 1904 the 'Cornish Riviera' began running non-stop from Paddington to Plymouth, Exeter being served by a slip coach and in the winter of 1906/7 reaching Exeter in 2hr 57min (58.8mile/hr) – what had been exceptional three years earlier, had become a day-to-day event, though the effort was not quite as good as that three years previously because in July 1906 most expresses were diverted from travelling via Bristol, to run over the newly-opened short cut via Westbury and Castle Cary which reduced the distance to Taunton and beyond by 20 miles. For reasons of economy from 23 September 1928 the 'Cornish Riviera' recommenced stopping at Exeter instead of slipping coaches. It took 2hr 55min (59.6mile/hr). By 1939 it reached Exeter in 2hr 49min (61.6mile/hr). During World War 2 with a load of 14 coaches, its allowance was increased to 3½hr, this being cut to 3¼hr on 1 October 1945. In 1968 the service was speeded to 2hr 19min (74.9mile/hr). The 1984 schedule of the 'Cornish Riviera', now an HST, is 2hr 3min (84.6mile/hr).

Before World War 1 the 'Torbay Express' was introduced with a 3hr non-stop run to Exeter and by World War 2 the time had been reduced to 2hr 49min. After World War 2 it ran a non-stop

Left:
The down 'Cornish Riviera Express' passes Cowley Bridge junction signalbox on 17 September 1960 behind a Type 4 'Warship' class diesel-hydraulic. *R. E. Toop*

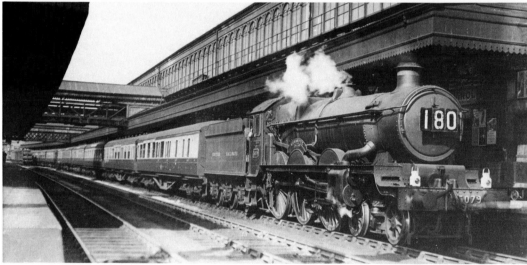

schedule of 3hr 3min to Exeter and a time of 2hr 41min (64.6mile/hr) in 1965. The 'Torbay Express' of today has lost its glamour, stopping at quite a few intermediate stations and taking 2hr 55min (59.5mile/hr), reaching Exeter only 19min before the 'Cornish Riviera' which leaves Paddington 75min later. The 'Torbay Express' takes 49min for the remaining 28¼ miles to Paignton. In 1964 the 'Golden Hind' was introduced with a 2hr 42min schedule (64.3mile/hr) to Exeter hauled by a 'Western' diesel-hydraulic kept in prime condition and hauling seven coaches. In 1972 it was accelerated to 2hr 28min (70.3mile/hr). That year it was also extended to Penzance offering a two hours later departure than ever before from London to principal stations in Cornwall, Penzance included.

In the summer of 1968 the service from Paddington to the West of England was re-shaped to run on an almost hourly basis to help promote travel to and from some of the railheads with

Top:
The 'Cornish Riviera Express', now formed of an IC125 set, enters platform 1 at St David's on 28 August 1984. The leading power car is No 43126 and the set is in the new Intercity livery. *Author*

Above:
'Castle' class No 5079 *Lysander* **stands at St David's with the down 'Torbay Express' on 14 April 1949. The locomotive is still in GWR livery but with 'British Railways' on the tender.**
J. H. Bamsey

growing traffic potential, particularly Exeter. The services used 10 or 12 coach train sets, each making at least one Paddington-Plymouth, or Paddington-Penzance round trip daily and in a few cases starting a third leg within 24hr. Four pairs of diesel-hydraulic 'Warships' provided 4,400hp to lead the crack trains. In 1972 the West of England service was put on a full hourly interval pattern of limited loads leaving at 30min past the hour, being odd hours from Plymouth departures and even hours for Torbay. IC125 High Speed Train services were introduced between Paddington and Penzance in the autumn of 1979. The 1984 timetable showed an hourly service to Plymouth with trains leaving at 45min past the hour, Torbay being generally served by a shuttle service from Newton or Exeter. Through trains run to

Birmingham at hourly intervals during the morning and early afternoon, such services going on variously to Aberdeen, Liverpool (Lime Street), Manchester (Piccadilly) and York, some of these being IC125s.

Top:
For many years the mainstay of West Country main line services were the Class 52 diesel-hydraulic 'Westerns'. No 1071 *Western Renown* leaves St David's with the 10.20 Plymouth-Paddington relief on 2 August 1971. *D. Wharton*

Above:
Over the level crossing at St David's comes No 1038 *Western Sovereign* with the 13.30 Paddington-Penzance service, composed mainly of Mk 2 stock, on 31 August 1972. *G. F. Gillham*

Today four named trains use St David's: the 'Cornish Riviera' Paddington-Penzance and its counterpart the 'Night Riviera' providing a sleeping car service to Exeter via Bristol taking 3hr 49min (50.8mile/hr) in 1984 but on Saturdays travelling by the direct route and taking 3hr 22min, while during the summer months it is supplemented by a Fridays-only non-sleeping car train leaving Paddington 2min earlier and also being routed via Bristol and reaching Temple Meads after the sleeper, though overtaking the sleeper at Plymouth and reaching Penzance first, the sleeper spending no less than 1hr 5min at Plymouth. The 'Mayflower' runs from Paddington to Plymouth taking 2hr 19min to Exeter and 1hr 3min onwards to its destination. In May 1984 the 09.20 ex Paddington and the 12.55 ex Paignton were christened the 'Torbay Express'. About 150 passenger trains serve St David's every 24hr. St David's is the ninth station on the Western Region in order of income from passenger revenue, issuing about ½ million tickets a year and about 1½ million people using the station annually, arriving, departing and changing.

The Saturday holiday traffic peak was reached in the 1950s. All holidaymakers to South Devon and Cornwall had to travel over the line between Exeter and Aller Junction, bifurcation point of the Torbay line. Apart from Saturdays-only trains to and from distant places such as Glasgow (St Enoch), Hull, Liverpool, Manchester, Newcastle-on-Tyne and Nottingham, many regular trains ran in two or more parts, some loaded to as many as 16 coaches. Twenty-four expresses went through Exeter before 8am, while between 9am and 4pm, 130 long-distance trains either stopped or passed through the station compared with a normal 24hr figure of 55 down WR and 22 SR, and 54 up WR and 24 SR. Although non-stop passenger trains could be routed over the goods lines which avoided the passenger station and trains halted there, in actual practice this rarely happened. On a summer Saturday St David's dealt with 8,000-10,000 passengers and issued over 4,000 tickets, half of which were cheap day returns.

Arrival or passing times of through expresses St David's. Summer Saturdays 1953, 10am-1pm.

DOWN		UP	
10.00W	11.43S	9.51W	11.42S
10.04S	11.47W	9.58W	11.43WN
10.06WN	11.54WN	10.03W	11.55WN
10.18S	11.59S	10.16WM	11.52S
10.21W	12.06W	10.21WN	12.00W
10.45WN	12.12S	10.28WN	12.05WN
10.51S	12.17W	10.39W	12.10WN
10.53W	12.27W	10.44WN	12.13S
11.03WN	12.31S	10.52WN	12.22WN
11.09WN	12.37W	11.07W	12.29S
11.15W	12.42WN	11.15W	12.31WN
11.17S	12.44S	11.19S	12.42WN
11.26S	12.49W	11.20WN	12.56W
11.28W	12.56WN	11.28WN	12.59S
11.39WN		11.29S	1.0WN
		11.35W	

W – Western Region
S – Southern Region
N – Non-stop

The opening LSWR service to Exeter in 1860 showed two trains arriving 6hr 50min after leaving Waterloo (25.1mile/hr), though from 1 August a faster train was put on taking 5hr 10min (33.2mile/hr). The following year 5 minutes was knocked off this schedule (33.8mile/hr), though to be fair to the LSWR, it must be pointed out that the route was still largely single line. The subsequent competition between the LSWR and the GWR has been recounted earlier. By August 1887 one train took 3hr 50min (44.8mile/hr) and in April 1910 3hr 15min (52.8mile/hr) which compared with the 'Cornish Riviera Limited Express' slip coach which arrived at Exeter 3hr after leaving Paddington (57.8mile/hr). In 1926 the SR named the 11am from Waterloo the 'Atlantic Coast Express' and at times this was the most multi-portioned train in the country, nine different sections being included in the formation. At the leading end of the train was an Ilfracombe portion of two third class brakes and a compo coach between, together with compo brakes for Torrington, Padstow, Bude and Plymouth. The first class restaurant car and kitchen car, and third class restaurant car had to be detached at Exeter, while three more compo brakes had been detached before the train reached Exeter. In the height of the summer season, two daily down services were run, on Saturdays these becoming no less than eight complete restaurant car trains departing from Waterloo between 10.24am and 12.5pm. The ACE averaged 3hr 2min (56.6mile/hr). The pre World War 2 winter timetable was based on regular interval restaurant car expresses leaving Waterloo for Exeter on weekdays at 9am, 11am (ACE), 1pm, 3pm and 6pm. The 1.30am newspaper express from Waterloo was the fastest Salisbury-Exeter train taking 94min for the 88 miles (56.1mile/hr). Up expresses left Exeter at 7.30am, 9.30am (Mondays only), 10.30am. 12.30pm (ACE), 2.30pm, 4.30pm, and 5.53pm. Cross country services were provided for Plymouth-Portsmouth coaches being attached to the 10.30am from Exeter, while a through Plymouth, Southampton, Brighton restaurant car train left Exeter at 1.5pm.

On 16 June 1947 the all Pullman 'Devon Belle' started from Waterloo with up to 10 cars for Ilfracombe and four for Plymouth. At first operating only at weekends, in 1949 it worked June-September Thursdays-Mondays inclusive in the down direction and Fridays-Tuesdays in the up. 1954 saw its withdrawal at the end of the season through lack of patronage. In 1950 the best

Top:
A feature of the 1950s was the operation of holiday expresses, passengers purchasing a ticket for several day excursions during one week. Here the 'City of Exeter Holiday Express' returns to St David's from Bude on 30 July 1958 behind 'T9' No 30709 and 'N' class No 31838.
T. Reardon

Above:
'West Country' Pacific No 34011 *Tavistock* in experimental light green livery shunts stock of the up 'Devon Belle' at Central station on 8 July 1949. *H. C. Casserley*

Below:
The observation car of the down 'Devon Belle' is seen passing Exmouth Junction on 8 July 1949. *H. C. Casserley*

Bottom:
The 8.15am Plymouth-Waterloo approaching St James' Park Halt on 12 April 1954 behind 'Merchant Navy' Pacific No 35022. *Holland-America Line.* *W. N. Lockett*

Top:
GWR 2-6-0 No 5376 and a 'West Country' Pacific on the down centre road at Exeter Central c1947. No 5376 will take forward the Plymouth portion of the 3.00pm ex Waterloo and the Pacific will take the Ilfracombe part.
Lens of Sutton

Above:
No 5376 again at Central, now in British Railways livery, having taken over the 6.47pm to Plymouth (3.00pm ex Waterloo) to familiarise Western Region crews with the route. On a Laira-based diagram the locomotive would have come up from Friary earlier in the day and have been serviced at Exmouth Junction. *M. E. J. Deane*

Waterloo-Exeter schedule was still 5min short of the 3¼hr attained by the LSWR 45 years earlier. The 11.47am Exeter to Plymouth (Friary) and the 4.40pm passengers and mail Plymouth - Eastleigh was worked as far as Exeter Central by a Western Region locomotive, usually a 2-6-0, but sometimes a 'Hall', and on 22 May 1963, No 4087 *Cardigan Castle*, to familiarise crews with the route in the event of a blockage of the WR main line. The 4.40pm stopped at virtually all stations. A WR engine also worked the 2.25pm Plymouth (Friary)-Exeter Central returning on the 6.47pm, the Plymouth portion of the 3.00pm Waterloo.

In 1963 it was planned to accelerate the 9am ex Waterloo to 2hr 48min (61.3mile/hr) including the Salisbury stop and hauling 11 coaches, but transfer to the WR stopped the plan being put into action. Although the line west of Salisbury was well used on summer Saturdays, taken as a whole its loss was great, weekday passenger traffic being relatively light, and freight hardly lucrative. In February 1964 it was announced that from 6

Below:
For several years the Class 42 'Warship' diesel-hydraulic locomotives dominated the Waterloo line service. No 811 *Daring* heads the 16.00 departure to Waterloo at platform 3 of St David's station on 1 September 1971. *J. H. Cooper-Smith*

Bottom:
From 1972 the 'Warships' were replaced by members of Class 33 on the Exeter-Waterloo line. No 33.008 passes St James' Park Halt with the 10.10 Exeter-Waterloo on 10 August 1976. *L. Bertram*

Above:
Eastleigh-based Class 33 No 33.023 leaves Exeter Central with the 13.45 St David's-Waterloo on 13 May 1984. *Hugh Ballantyne*

Below:
Successor to the Class 33s on the Waterloo route, Class 50 No 50.033 *Glorious* at platform 3, St David's with the 12.20 to Waterloo on 28 August 1984. *Author*

September 1964 the Waterloo and West of England trains would be semi-fasts and were to terminate at Exeter, Devon and Cornwall being served by DMUs. The 11am ex-Waterloo, the former ACE, was terminated at Salisbury, but so many passengers travelled on it, believing it still to be the ACE, that the Brighton-Plymouth train at Salisbury had to be strengthened by four coaches and on at least one Saturday, the 11am was sent on to Exeter. In 1984 nine through trains run from Waterloo, an early morning one leaving at 01.40 also conveying newspapers and those in the

Salisbury   Andover
Basingstoke   Woking
London   Waterloo
→

Top:
No 50.033 *Glorious* **again, picking its way through the pointwork, arrives at St David's with the 06.50 from Waterloo on 28 August 1984.** *Author*

Above:
Board at St David's identifying a Waterloo service. 28 August 1984. *Author*

daytime at 09.10 and ten minutes past the odd hours until 19.10, the 15.10 being the fastest and taking 3hr 21min. Up trains are not run on a regular interval basis. In addition to the expresses, there are two DMU workings from Exeter to Honiton and back.

Returning to the SDR, with the opening to Teignmouth, seven trains ran each way taking 45min and when the line was extended to Laira in 1848, trains were allowed 2hr 15min, and 2hr 20min to Millbay the following year. Speeds over the SDR were slow, but in view of the number of stations at which expresses were required to stop, coupled with the curves and the gradients which were as severe as 1 in 36, the speeds were quite reasonable. The mail trains begun 1 February 1855 took 2hr 25min for the 52¾ miles, but by 1865 times had been cut to 1hr 45min. In July 1877 the fastest train took 2hr, though competition from the LSWR which had reached the city the previous year, caused the 'Zulu' to be put on which covered the distance in 1hr 41min. In 1890 the 'Cornishman' cut this to 1½hr, reduced in 1901 to 1hr 22min and two years later to 1hr 20min. Modern motive power has speeded trains up the banks, but curves still restrict downhill speeds. In 1984 the 'Cornish Riviera' was given 57min from Exeter (54.7mile/hr) and 3hr from London (75.2mile/hr), whereas in 1957 it took 4hr Paddington-Plymouth (56.4mile/hr). One interesting feature of the Exeter-Newton local service was that it was virtually non-existent on summer Saturdays as all the paths were appropriated by longer distance trains.

The Kingswear line had gradients as steep as 1 in 55. In August 1887 the service gave 11 trains each

Above:
The down 'Devonian' approaches St David's on 20 July 1956, behind 'Castle' class No 5053 *Earl Cairns* and 'Hall' No 6917 *Oldlands Hall*. Class E1/R 0-6-2T No 32135 awaits its next banking duty. Cadbury's Exeter depot can be seen behind No 5053. *R. C. Riley*

way daily, and 15 in April 1910. In 1957, 19 trains ran through to Kingswear Mondays-Fridays plus 22 short workings to Paignton, while on summer Saturdays the numbers increased to 20 and 33 respectively, through trains running to Birmingham (Moor Street); Manchester (London Road); Sheffield (Midland) and Wolverhampton Low Level. Since January 1973 Paignton has been the end of the line for BR, with the Paignton-Kingswear section operated by the Dart Valley Railway Co as the Torbay Steam Railway. Today 20 trains run daily, most being second class only DMUs working a shuttle service from Newton, though one is an IC125 from Bradford Interchange and one the 'Torbay Express' from Paddington. On summer Saturdays the service is increased to 31 down trains, three through services running from Bradford Interchange; two from Birmingham; one from Carlisle; one from Crewe; one from Liverpool; three from Manchester Piccadilly; five from Newcastle; two from Nottingham; one from Preston and one from York.

In 1887 the Exe Valley branch had five trains between Exeter and Dulverton, the fastest taking 1hr 6min for the 24¾ miles, the service in 1910 being similar though with one more train. In September 1937 the service consisted of seven trains each way plus five short workings Exeter-Tiverton, taking 1hr 10min to Dulverton, but with five extra stops. In 1957 the summer service showed 10 trains throughout and two short workings.

The Teign Valley had an opening service of four trains each way Exeter-Heathfield taking about 1½hr for the 17 miles, increased to five trains by 1910 and six by 1928 taking 1hr, this service altering very little either in frequency or timing. The final timetable, which was for the winter of 1957/58 was revolutionary, giving better locomotive and stock working as some trains ran through to and from the Exe Valley, though not advertised as such, and involved at least one working for a Newton Abbot 45xx Prairie tank. Because of the procession of main line trains full of holidaymakers on summer Saturdays, during the holiday peak in 1957 for instance, two branch trains terminated and started at Alphington Halt, passengers being left to make their own way to and from Exeter by Corporation bus, the timetable warning that 'heavy luggage not conveyed', while another terminated at St Thomas, running empty to St. David's.

Below:
Class 50 No 50.039 *Implacable* entering St David's with the 09.36 departure from Liverpool Lime Street on 28 August 1984. *Author*

Bottom:
Collett 0-4-2T No 1450 leaving the bay platform at St David's with the Exe Valley train on 21 September 1963. *R. A. Lumber*

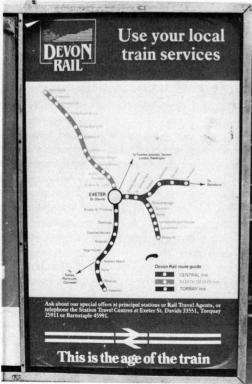

Left:
Devon Rail map, 1984. *Author*

The Exeter & Crediton opened with seven trains daily each way, while the North Devon Railway's first service was four weekday trains taking 1hr 50min between Exeter and Barnstaple. In 1887 seven trains ran from Exeter-Ilfracombe, the fastest taking 2hr 4min for the 54¾ miles, while eight trains ran Exeter-Torrington, a distance of 54 miles, the fastest taking 1hr 47min. In 1910 seven ran to Ilfracombe, the quickest taking 1hr 54min and seven trains to Torrington, the fastest reaching there in 1¾hr. In 1957 eight through trains ran between Exeter and Ilfracombe daily with 13 on summer Saturdays, those to Plymouth being 11 Mondays-Saturdays. In 1984 nine trains ran between Exeter and Barnstaple, the fastest covering the 39 miles from St David's in 55min omitting five of the 11 intermediate stops (42.5mile/hr). One train ran through from Paignton;

two ran through to Paignton; one to Exmouth and on Sundays through trains ran from Barnstaple to Exmouth (2) and Plymouth (1).

The North Devon Railway Action Committee was formed late in 1962 before the publication of *The Reshaping of British Railways*, the Beeching Plan. It recommended that the train service should be reduced to six trains daily, but speeds increased and connections at Exeter improved. If through coaches to and from Waterloo continued, the report said priority should be given to the despatch from Exeter of the North Devon, rather than the Plymouth section, the only North Devon train having such priority being the ACE. It pointed out the importance of the Plymouth section was a relic

Left:
The cab of No 51307, rear car of a Class 118 three-car DMU forming the 13.58 St David's-Barnstaple on 28 August 1984. *Author*

Below:
Rear view of DMU No P465 leaving St David's as the 11.18 to Barnstaple, 28 August 1984. Although not brought into use until several months later, some of the new colour light signals are already in place. *Author*

Above:
Five lines occupied at St David's on 28 August 1984. From left to right: empty coaching stock, the 13.58 Exeter-Barnstaple, DMU empty coaching stock, No 43164 leading the 12.50 Plymouth-Paddington HST, a relief up Paddington headed by No 50.038 out of picture. *Author*

of competition between the LSWR and the GWR. A census held on 7 May 1963 found the average number of passengers on trains between station stops to be 22.09.

A survey in 1975 showed rather surprisingly that over 75% of passengers on the branch were using the service to feed into and out of the Inter-City network, only 16% actually making trips between Exeter and Barnstaple as such, and less than ten per cent beginning or ending their journeys at one of the intermediate stations. In 1984 about 50 commuters used the line daily.

The opening service from Exeter-Exmouth was five each way including Sundays, this being an unusual feature as most lines had less trains on the Sabbath. Trains took 30min for the distance of 10½ miles. By August 1887 the service had increased to 10 down and 11 up trains with five on Sundays. By August 1905 a train ran non-stop leaving Exmouth at 9.30am and arrived at Queen Street 18min later.

From 1 June 1908 in addition to the 18 trains each way between Exeter and Exmouth, a railmotor service was introduced between Exeter and Topsham making 10 trips daily each way and five on Sundays.

The SR began in 1923 with 20 down and 21 up trains throughout the length of the branch. In the summer of 1932 the 7.48am up was booked through to Plymouth, curiously running into Platform 1 Bay at Queen Street. In September 1937 an intensive service of 27 trains ran in each direction with 19 on Sundays. A half-hourly service ran for part of the day, these leaving Exeter or Exmouth at 15 or 45 minutes past the hour, catering for the needs of commuters, students, schoolchildren, shoppers, the military, holidaymakers and excursionists. On summer Sundays, short notice specials nicknamed 'Sandhoppers' trains would be arranged by Exeter Control to clear platforms of trippers bound for Exmouth, running in 'Q' paths in the timetable, with similar arrangements when homeward bound in the evening. Owing to the length of platforms, branch trains were limited to seven bogies.

In 1951, 24 trains ran on weekdays increasing to 26 on summer Saturdays, while the Sunday service

Above:
'M7' class 0-4-4T No 35 approaches Polsloe Bridge halt with an Exmouth-Exeter train on 21 May 1935. *H. C. Casserley*

Below:
Adams '02' class 0-4-4T No 30232 and BR standard 2-6-2T No 82017 leaving Exeter Central for Exmouth on 29 June 1957. *R. C. Riley*

was 13. Trains were allowed about 26min for the distance with a ½min stop at the majority of stations, though 1-1½min at Polsloe Bridge Halt which is indicative of its traffic. In the summer of 1957 no less than 30 trains ran on weekdays and 17 on Sundays plus a Polsloe Bridge Halt-Exmouth train to handle the heavy tripper traffic originating there.

On 4 January 1960 the non-stop evening express was re-introduced taking 19min for the run – 1min more than when it was introduced in 1905, but was accelerated to its old schedule from 14 June 1960. It owed its re-instatement to Charles Williams, Divisional Traffic Superintendent at Exeter Control who aimed to hold the substantial number of people who already travelled by train and also win back passengers who were beginning to feel that road travel had its disadvantages. 14 June 1963 was the last day of operation of the lunchtime train to Topsham, put on mainly for the benefit of workers at or near Exeter Central and the remnant of the railmotor service.

The branch was dieselised on 9 September 1963, some trains being diagrammed to work through to St David's and through services being advertised: 7.15am Exmouth-Plymouth; 9.15am to Kingswear

and 7.15pm to Newton, while the evening non-stop scheduled a record 17min. The winter of 1964-65 saw a reduction in the weekday service to 25 down trains and on 3 October 1966, seven trains were withdrawn as an economy measure. From 3 May 1976 all stopping trains served St James' Park Halt and the newly-opened Lympstone Commando which added 1 and 2min respectively to the running time, increasing the overall schedule to 26min down and 27 up. From May 1977 nearly all trains ran through to St David's. In 1984 22 trains ran on weekdays and 13 on Sundays, the service being second class only. The branch provides the major flow of rail commuters to Exeter, 95% using Central station.

In 1949 the 9.18am Saturdays only Exmouth-Manchester was introduced, a WR engine being booked to take over from the branch tank engine at Central. The SR timetable published the train as

Below:
DMU No P469 on the 10.55 from Exmouth arriving at St David's on 28 August 1984. A tractor unit with BRUTE vehicles is waiting to cross. *Author*

terminating at Central, while the WR advertised it as an Exeter St David's-Manchester train, but despite the apparent confusion between the two regions' publicity, it was known locally as a through Exmouth-Manchester service. It was not until 1963 when the branch came under WR jurisdiction that it was officially advertised for its last four years as running through to Manchester from Exmouth.

Top:
The 9.18am Saturdays only Exmouth-Manchester composed of a mixture of former GWR and LMS coaches arrives at St David's behind No 6959 *Peatling Hall* on 5 August 1950. *T. Reardon*

Above:
Ex-LSWR coaches previously in use as camping coaches at sites in East Devon are seen at Exmouth Junction on 18 September 1965. *R. A. Lumber*

Development of Freight Services

In GWR times, express goods trains had picturesque names such as:

10.55pm Bristol-Laira – 'The Drake'
11.00am Exeter-Pontypool Road – 'The Ponty'
4.00pm Exeter-Old Oak Common – 'The Flying Pig'
4.58pm Marazion-Bristol – 'The Tre, Pol and Pen'
5.30pm Newton Abbot-Paddington – 'The Hackney'
9.32pm Old Oak Common-Penzance – 'The Cornishman'
10.10pm Paddington-Laira – 'The Tamar'
11.35pm Paddington-Newton Abbot – 'The Devonshireman'
2.50pm Penzance-Paddington – 'The Search Light'
5.40am Pontypool Road-Newton Abbot – 'The Laira'
10.30pm Reading-Laira – 'The Biscuit'
3.50pm Swindon-Tavistock Junction – 'The Rasher'
9.33pm Westbury-Penzance – 'Western Flash'

The first regular GWR narrow gauge goods worked to Exeter from March 1876. The timetable for December 1881 stated that up narrow gauge trains were to be marshalled in the following order:
'Wagons for Bristol should in all cases be next to the engine. Next to these the empties (GWR). Next the Trucks for the Midland Line. The Wagons for G W Trains via Standish Junction; and last of all the Trucks for the G W Line between Bristol and Paddington, those for the latter Station to stand last, and the others in Station order – Keynsham first and so on'.

In 1907 goods trains were made up at St David's for Bristol and the north; Cardiff, London, Plymouth

Below:
War Department 2-8-0 No 77421 on the goods avoiding lines with a down freight passing St David's on 2 October 1948. *J. H. Bamsey*

and Penzance; while they arrived from Bristol, Kingswear, London, Manchester and the north, Penzance, Plymouth and South Wales; altogether some 60 goods, cattle, coal and empty stock trains using St David's every 24hr, in addition to about 40 LSWR goods trains which passed through. Goods staff in 1907 numbered 70-80 men. Exeter was the headquarters of the goods district extending from below Bristol to the Brixham, Dartmouth and

Above:
Type 3 'Hymek' diesel No D7018 passes Exeter with a down freight on 2 July 1963. *R. C. Riley*

Below:
Class 31 No 31.286 with a short air-braked freight on the down through road at St David's on 28 August 1984. *Author*

Moretonhampstead branches. The district goods manager's offices were at 95 Queen Street in the heart of the city.

In 1940 the SR ran three principal express freights each way: the 7.38pm from Exeter Central goods yard, and the 8.37pm and 10.40pm from Exmouth Junction marshalling yard. Thirteen services from the west radiated on Exeter, the 7.38pm conveying goods from these trains to the London markets. The 8.37pm was a continuation of the 12.45pm ex Torrington and conveyed general traffic for London, and livestock and perishable traffic for the Midlands via Templecombe and the Somerset & Dorset. The 10.42pm was a continuation of the 4.52pm ex Torrington. Down trains consisted of the 10.20pm Nine Elms-Plymouth which conveyed traffic only to Exeter and the west thereof, the 9.32pm Nine Elms-Torrington picked up traffic for St David's at Salisbury, while the 10.47pm Nine Elms-Exmouth Junction carried traffic for East Devon stations. All these trains had 27ton bogie brake vans on the rear. The maximum

Left:
Adams '380' class 4-4-0 No 383 at the north end of St David's c1902.
R. S. Carpenter collection

Below:
Drummond 700 class 'Black Motor' No 30691 passes St James' Park halt with an up mixed freight for Exmouth Junction in the late 1950s.
R. A. Lumber

Above:
Drummond Class 700 No 30691 is assisted out of St David's with a lengthy freight by Standard 2MT No 82013 for the 1 in 37 incline up to Central station on 26 July 1960.
Frank Church

load of the three up trains was 50 wagons from Exeter-Templecombe including 15 vacuum braked wagons 'inside the engine'. Freight traffic on the Exeter-Salisbury line was relatively light, the only heavy goods being ballast trains from Meldon Quarry and the main coal traffic was that consumed by SR locomotives. Freight trains were handled by Pacifics or Class S15 4-6-0s. The inclusion of goods trains in the same working diagrams as passenger trains was common throughout the district, so that an engine working outwards on a goods duty, often had to be at its turn round point punctually in order to return home with a passenger train.

The accent on freight at Exeter is that it was and still is a major distribution centre. In pre-railway days it was distribution from the docks; in the railway era it is distribution from centralised depots. Until about 20 years ago, a wide variety of goods arrived by rail: engineering products, builders' supplies, petrol, coal, stock for retail shops, and foodstuffs for farm animals. There were four main areas for handling freight: Alphington Road Goods Depot; the City Basin; Riverside and Exeter Central, while Exmouth Junction dealt with the marshalling of SR trains to and from the west.

Alphington Road Goods Depot opened 1 July 1903 by the Exeter Railway which was requested by the GWR to provide accommodation for a heavy tonnage of coal traffic as a response to the numerous applications it received from merchants. Rail access was by a steeply descending curving line, trailing from the Teign Valley branch. The depot had four sidings, one of which served the goods shed and another the cattle dock. In December 1960 three sidings, together with the goods shed and cattle dock were removed for building a new warehouse, but at the time of writing, the warehouse is no longer in use. The depot closed 4 December 1967. The loop line is currently used for storing bitumen tank wagons. At the west end of the run round loop two sidings on a descending gradient of 1 in 42 were opened on 19 October 1939 the same year as the cattle market. The two platforms allowed 28 cattle vans to be

Above:

Class 33 No 33.059 arrives at Exeter Central with ballast empties on 13 May 1984. *Hugh Ballantyne*

loaded simultaneously. Eighteen pens were provided on the cattle sidings, as many as 500-600 beasts being loaded on Fridays and up to 100 on Mondays. A meat platform was built to serve a planned abattoir, though due to the city council's change of policy, it was never used. These sidings were worked from the City Basin Junction signalbox and caused the City Basin Junction ground frame to be taken out of use from 19 October 1939. With the carriage of cattle being taken over by road transport, the cattle market sidings were lifted in 1972.

Although it was the original proposal of both the Exeter & Crediton and the B&E to terminate their lines at the canal basin, this intention was in fact never carried out and later regretted by Exeter Corporation. In 1849 the latter's surveyor suggested two possible schemes for a rail connection and also proposed that it could be linked to St David's by an inclined plane on which would work five-ton boats equipped with wheels. Finally after traders complained at the cost of double transhipment between the City Basin and St David's, the corporation strongly pressurised the SDR into building a docks branch. A broad gauge line 34ch in length, it was opened 17 June 1867

from a trailing junction off the SDR down line to the City Basin, access to the quayside being by wagon turntable. The Act, 28 and 29 Vic c 255 of 5 July 1865, stipulated that the branch should be of mixed gauge and that narrow gauge rails be laid on the main line from St David's station to the junction for use by LSWR traffic. This was not carried out until 20 March 1871 and then as the third rail was laid on the down line only, the daily City Basin train consisted of wagons of both gauges and linked by a match truck with extra wide buffers and a coupling chain sliding on a transverse bar at either end. On returning the train had of necessity to go up the down line for 1½ miles. This was the only mixed gauge section on the SDR. Apart from private sidings agreements, the City Basin line closed to goods on 6 September 1965. As well as serving the basin, the branch also served the gas works, but due to changing over to North Sea gas, rail traffic was discontinued and the private siding agreement terminated on 23 November 1973, while the line to the Central Electricity Generating Board's works had already ceased by that date. Before commencing shunting at the CEGB siding, the guard and shunter were required to satisfy themselves that the coal unloading shute was not fouling the line. A traverser was provided to facilitate the movement of wagons to the required siding and this had to be locked in position for the straight road before BR could bring in a train. As a wagon tippler was used for discharge, all wagons, whether fitted with grease or oil axle boxes, were required to be examined by a C&W Examiner to ensure that the oil boxes were replenished and a general examination made to find any displaced planks or damaged axle guards. This procedure also had to be carried out on wagons leaving the gas board's siding as a wagon tippler was used there. Because of the four level crossings on the City Basin branch, a train working on it was required to be accompanied by a shunter and porter from St Thomas', the latter being responsible for unlocking and re-locking the crossing gates. The porter, equipped with a red flag, protected Haven Road level crossing.

In October 1966 two sidings were laid to serve the Texaco Oil Distribution Depot and 10-20 oil tanks from Avonmouth arriving on 3-4 days each week by special train, were taken to the sidings in the afternoon and removed empty that same evening. As the empties had to be propelled to the main line and the engine driver was unable to sight the stop signal, a repeater signal was installed which worked off the same lever. It was unique, being painted as a distant signal, but being square-ended. Texaco ceased having rail deliveries with the closure of their Exeter Distribution Depot circa 1979 and the siding closed on 21 July 1983,

Below:
Ex-GWR '5700' class 0-6-0PT No 3629 shunting at the City Basin on 1 October 1958. *R. A. Lumber*

Right:
Class 45 No 45.035 with a Texaco oil train branching off at Exeter City Basin signalbox on 4 June 1976. *Col M. H. Cobb*

Below right:
No 45.035 passes the unusual repeater signal on the City Basin branch in June 1976.
Col M. H. Cobb

the direct connection with Exeter Basin Junction being lifted later that year but reinstated in 1984.

A low level loop line, opened 1 July 1903, made a direct connection between the Teign Valley line and the City Basin, this line now being continuously occupied by bitumen wagons being unloaded and additional to the siding opened for the purpose in April 1929. Today King's Asphalt takes delivery of 8-12 tanks a day, increasing in summer, as more road tarring is carried out during this season, the terminal acting as a bitumen centre for a large part of Devon. Exeter City Basin signalbox was usually open 08.00-16.00 only, wages being partly paid by King's Asphalt.

In March 1958 the stub of the Teign Valley line threw off a trailing branch to the Marsh Barton Trading Estate. The Cadbury/Fry siding closed in 1971 while E. Pearse & Co's siding has not been used for about two years because of the collapse of the export steel market.

Below:
The City Basin branch on the right and Alphington Road yard on the left, 6 August 1984. *Author*

Bottom:
Class 08 diesel shunter No 08.937 with empty asphalt wagons from Kings Asphalt approaching St David's on 28 August 1984. *Author*

Top:
A Class 08 shunts tankers at Riverside yard on 6 August 1984. *Author*

Above:
Unloading cement at Cowley Loop sidings on 6 August 1984. *Author*

Riverside, north of St David's station, is one of the Speedlink yards and traffic off main line freights from the Severn Tunnel Junction yard has to be sorted for Barnstaple, Newton Abbot, Heathfield, Exmouth Junction, Exeter Central, City Basin, Whimple and Pinhoe, and vice versa; in fact

Riverside is now the South West's main marshalling yard. Another important part of the yard's workload is marshalling departmental trains for midweek and weekend engineering work and dealing with trains to and from Meldon Quarry.

The large timber built goods shed immediately north west of St David's was latterly used by National Carriers for parcels traffic and more recently for storing MAS equipment. The brick built former broad/narrow gauge transfer shed was used for lorry/van loads of sacks and large consignments, and the siding behind for loading outwards sugar beet and potatoes. Until April 1984

Above:
'West County' Pacific No 34092 *City of Wells* passing St James' Park Halt with an up ballast train from Meldon Quarry on 18 April 1964. *R. A. Lumber*

wagon repairs were carried out by a private firm behind the transfer shed. Opposite Riverside is New Yard which dealt only with full wagon loads and included a Bibby's cattle cake distribution depot. Today New Yard is used by the remaining full load freight customers in the Exeter area. Four nights a week an empty cement train leaves Riverside Yard for Westbury. A down loop siding is provided from Cowley Bridge Junction to St David's and often a stone train from Meldon Quarry can be seen standing there. The quarry, the only one owned by BR, is being developed and traffic has increased to up to six trains daily. A minimum of about 20 freight trains run through Exeter daily.

In the days when brake vans were obligatory on goods trains, the following side lamps were required to be exhibited between Middle and West boxes:

Line	Nearside	Offside
Down platform	Red	White
Down through	Red	Red
Down middle platform	White	Red
Up middle platform	White	Red
Up main platform	Red	Red
Up relief	Red	White

Two brake vans are provided at Exeter for local use,

none being required for main line work as the area west of Taunton is for fully fitted freight trains only. Their sole purpose today is for carrying a travelling shunter and guard since 08 cabs are cramped and only allow for the driver and second man. Because their one use is for carrying personnel, they can be placed at any position in the train. Such a brake van is required on trips from Riverside to City Basin, Central, Exmouth Junction and Pinhoe.

The goods depot at Queen Street was in two halves, the goods shed and one yard being north of the passenger station, with two small subsidiary yards on either side of the steeply descending line west of the passenger platforms. A feature of these latter yards were wagon turntables serving stub sidings where motive power was horses and men's muscles. The sidings south of the main line were remodelled 17 March 1931 abolishing the turntables, but those on the north side remained until taken out of use in September 1969. A coal wharf adjoined the carriage shed at the east end of the station, with a cattle dock on the opposite side of the main lines. These various sidings at Central

Top:
Class 08 No 08.937 descends the bank into St David's past Exeter West signalbox with empty Blue Circle Cement wagons from Central station on 28 August 1984. *Author*

Above:
Unloading beer from Speedlink service wagons, Premier Transport dock, Exeter Central, 7 August 1984. *Author*

were served by four daily transfer trips in each direction to and from Exmouth Junction which in 1951 received two daily transfers from, and one to,

St David's. The Central depot, closed to general goods traffic on 4 December 1967, is now the principal Blue Circle Cement distribution centre in Devon, receiving up to four block trains of cement in Presflo wagons from the Blue Circle Cement Works at Westbury run on four days a week and consisting of 20-25 Presflos to each train. The cement is road hauled from Exeter to other parts of Devon. Central also has a dock used by Premier Transport who, on behalf of BR, provide a collection and delivery service for general freight traffic passing on Speedlink services, the major

Above:
Exmouth Junction looking east, with the concrete works in the centre and sidings to the right. *Western Fuels Ltd*

traffic being beer from Park Royal delivered to Devon and Cornwall from this terminal. Central Yard is served by two or three freight trips from and to Riverside each weekday.

Exmouth Junction marshalling yard a mile east of Central, consisted of 10 parallel roads, the shunting neck doubling as the up goods reception and also the down goods departure road before the eight road down yard was built. In 1951 Exmouth Junction yard handled about 700 wagons daily, with 30 goods trains departing and 27 arriving. Nearly all trains from the London direction had to be shunted at Exmouth Junction and new trains formed for despatch to Plymouth, North Devon, North Cornwall and Exmouth and also for transfer to the WR at St David's. Conversely, wagons arriving at Exmouth Junction from these places had to be shunted into trains for Yeovil Junction, Templecombe, Salisbury and London. No public facilities were provided for loading and unloading, all local freight traffic being dealt with at Exeter Central goods depot.

A coal concentration depot was opened on 4 December 1967, the closure date of Central to goods, on the site of Exmouth Junction concrete works, to serve as the coal railhead for the whole of Devon, onwards conveyance being by road transport. In January 1984 it received approximately 30 vacuum braked wagons weekly, or six of the new high capacity air braked wagons, but this figure is likely to fall as the domestic market for coal is still shrinking. Six thousand to 8,000 tons arrive for stacking May-October, while coal merchants take away a similar tonnage for stacking in their own yards, the annual throughput on the concentration depot being in the region of 50,000 tons. Western Fuels Ltd rent four sidings from BR, two of which have an underground discharge pit for coal dropping from hopper wagons, while a short siding is used for wagon storage and a long one for empties. 56-ton PBA bogie covered hopper wagons owned by Tiger Railcar Leasing (UK) Ltd and operating for English China Clays are cleaned there on contract by Beckett Steamcleaning Services. This operation is carried out with a mild acid concrete cleaner which eats into the deposits of china clay which are then removed by steam.

Top:
Exmouth Junction coal concentration depot, with hopper wagons standing over conveyor belts. *Western Fuels Ltd*

Above:
Exmouth Junction coal concentration depot, coal conveyor belt. *Western Fuels Ltd*

Right:
Beckett Steamcleaning Services cleaning an ECC Tiger bogie china clay wagon at Exmouth Junction coal concentration depot on 7 August 1984. *Author*

Above:
The grain silo and brick siding at Pinhoe in a down view on 7 August 1984. *Author*

On the up side between the site of the former Whipton Bridge Halt and Pinhoe are three sidings 2 miles 41ch from Central, serving a grain silo having incoming loaded grain wagons and outgoing loaded trucks, about two weekly, from Westbrick. Until the private siding agreement was terminated on 6 September 1965 the same turnout from the main line served two sidings to the Poltimore Brick Co. Further east a siding was put in about 1942 to a Ministry of Food cold store, the agreement terminated 1 October 1967, the siding taken out of use in 1969, reinstated as Continental (London) Ltd and removed March 1979. From the down line a siding 2 miles 27ch from Central was opened to Pye Storage Ltd in September 1953 and taken out of use on 23 March 1968.

A short distance down the Exmouth branch was the New Siding, 1mile 20ch from Central, situated on the west side of the line and serving the Exeter Brick & Tile Co, later the Western Counties Brick Co at its northern end, and the Domestic Chemical Co, opened in July 1921 as Collard's siding, at its southern end. Access was by a trailing connection off the up line operated from Exmouth Junction signalbox which also controlled a trailing crossover between the up and down branch lines immediately south of the siding to enable goods trains from Exmouth Junction to gain the correct road when proceeding towards Exmouth. Traffic to and from the siding circulated via Exmouth Junction yard and comprised outgoing bricks and ingoing chemicals for repacking, subsequent distribution being by road. Curiously the siding was the responsibility of the Topsham stationmaster, although Polsloe Bridge Halt nearer Topsham was under the jurisdiction of Exeter Central. The brick siding agreement terminated 12 May 1967 and the chemical siding was taken out of use 7 January 1973. Beyond the site of these sidings the double track now becomes single.

Motive Power Scene

The B&E at first was worked by the GWR, but in 1849 its financial position was such that it became completely independent and bought its own locomotives and rolling stock. James Pearson, formerly the engineer in charge of the atmospheric section of the SDR, was appointed locomotive superintendent of the B&E in May 1850, his headquarters being at Exeter where temporary repair shops had been erected. In February 1851 C. H. Gregory, chief engineer, reported that 'The Contract Drawings are completed for the Permanent Workshops at Exeter, suitable for carrying on the whole repairs of your Locomotive Establishment'. Shortly afterwards the directors changed their minds, almost certainly on Pearson's advice, and told the shareholders in August that they had unanimously decided on building the workshops at Bristol, these being eventually opened in September 1854. The B&E began its working existence with 28 of Gooch's locomotives, but subsequent engines were designed by Pearson. The B&E having a relatively short main line of only 76 miles, tended to use tank engines, the most impressive examples being 4-2-4 express tank locomotives with flangeless 9ft driving wheels. These were the fastest engines of their period, the highest recorded maximum speed reached by them being 81.8mile/hr. They were quite economical burning less than 22lb of coke per mile. 4-4-0STs were also used for main line passenger duties, other tank engines being of the 2-2-2T, 2-2-2WT, 0-6-0ST and 0-4-0WT wheel arrangements, the latter designed for shunting. Tender engines comprised those of the 4-2-2, 0-6-0 and 2-4-0 types.

As the atmospheric system was not ready initially and then proved unreliable, from the time of opening the first section between Exeter and Teignmouth the SDR was mainly dependent on an agreement with the GWR for working its traffic, though the available engines were far from an ideal choice for the 1 in 36 gradients. Passenger trains were hauled either by 'Fire Fly' class 2-2-2s with 7ft driving wheels, similar engines of the 'Sun' class with 6ft driving wheels, or the 'Leo' class 2-4-0s with 5ft coupled wheels, while for freight duties 0-6-0s of the 'Hercules' class with 5ft driving wheels were used, these being the only broad gauge 0-6-0s to have outside sandwich frames and the least unsatisfactory engines on the SDR. From 1 July 1851 Messrs Edward Evans & Charles Geach won the 10 year contract for providing 12 4-4-0 locomotives and four 0-6-0STs, the contractors charging rather less than the temporary arrangement made with the GWR. In 1859 the contract was renewed for seven years with Messrs Edward Evans, Thomas Walker and Daniel Gooch, Charles Geach, an ironmaster of Birmingham having died. During this period of the second contract, 16 4-4-0s of the 'Hawk' class and eight 0-6-0STs were added to the stock. On 1 July 1866 the SDR took over locomotive working and also that of the Cornwall Railway and West Cornwall Railway. The SDR found that this reduced running costs from an average of 1s 6½d per train-mile to 9¾d showing that the clear profit to the contractors had been very nearly 50%. The first engines ordered by the SDR were six 'Pluto' class 4-4-0STs, the first SDR tank engines to have inside plate frames. Two goods 0-6-0STs *Romulus* and *Remus* were also ordered. Like those on the Great Western, SDR engines bore only names until taken over by the GWR on 1 February 1876. The last engines for the SDR were ten 0-6-0ST convertible goods engines of the 'Buffalo' class; four 4-4-0ST passenger engines of the 'Leopard' class together with three 0-4-0WTs and five 0-4-0STs for dock shunting at Plymouth. *Achilles*, then nameless, lasted until 1932. One interesting feature of the stock was that almost all SDR passenger engines carried the sand box on top of the saddle tank, while the goods engines carried it in front of the smoke box. Soon after amalgamation with the GWR, ten GWR 'Hawthorn' class 2-4-0 tender engines were converted to saddle tanks for service west of Exeter. To work the 'Cornishman' which ran non-stop between Exeter and Plymouth, three Dean 2-4-0 side tank engines were converted to

Above:
'Bulldog' class 4-4-0 No 3335 on the through road at St David's on 27 July 1948. *W. Potter*

Below:
A classic GWR scene at St David's station. A four-cylinder Churchward 'Star' class locomotive heads a rake of clerestory stock on a down service.
L&GRP courtesy David & Charles

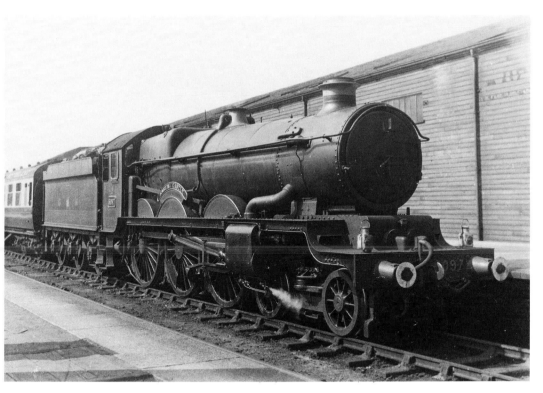

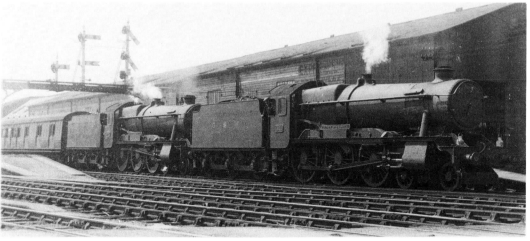

Top:
'Castle' class No 5097 *Sarum Castle* with an up express at St David's on 27 July 1948. *W. Potter*

Above:
The rather unusual combination of two 'County' class 4-6-0s, Nos 1011 *County of Chester* and 1028 *County of Warwick* on a Paddington train leaving St David's on 27 July 1948. *W. Potter*

tender engines so that sufficient water could be carried for the trip.

Representatives of most of the Great Western locomotive classes have worked through Exeter. The introduction of the 'Duke' class 4-4-0 in 1895 meant that for the first time engines could run through from Paddington to Plymouth without changing at Newton or Exeter. In addition to working passenger trains to Cornwall, they were also utilised on fast goods from Paddington to Exeter. The influence of Churchward appeared in

Top:
Collett 'King' class locomotive No 6018 *King Henry VI* approaches St David's station in June 1951 with a royal train from Cornwall to London. *T. Reardon*

Above:
Massive '4700' class 2-8-0 No 4703, usually an express freight locomotive, heads a down passenger service at St David's. This class was regularly used on passenger trains on busy summer Saturdays. *T. Reardon*

the 'Bulldog' and 'Atbara' classes, while in the early 1900s the 'Cities' were renowned for their speed exploits on Plymouth-Paddington trains. Shortly afterwards, two cylinder 'Saints' and four cylinder 'Stars' came on the scene, later to be eclipsed by 'Castles' and 'Kings'. On summer Saturdays mixed traffic 'Halls' and 'Granges' which had probably been hauling goods trains during the week, appeared on the many holiday trains, as did the

unique '4700' class 2-8-0s. Tank engines of the
2-4-0T and 0-4-2T variety worked local passenger
trains, while during the era when steam railmotors
were in favour, some were shedded at Exeter to
work trains to Dawlish Warren and on the Teign
Valley branch. When enthusiasm for these vehicles
died down and their disadvantages were found to
outweigh their advantages, they were replaced by
0-4-2Ts of the '4800' class. 2-6-2Ts also appeared as
did 0-6-0PTs of the various classes, the latter
rostered on passenger, goods and shunting turns.
In 1951 one of the two 'Castles' shedded at Exeter
worked a complicated two-day diagram alternately
with a Bristol 'Castle', involving the 9.7am Exeter
Bristol; the 5.25pm Bristol-Paddington; the
10.10pm Paddington-Bristol; 9.5am Bristol-Cardiff;
12.35pm Cardiff-Kingswear and the 6.25pm
Kingswear-Exeter. The other 'Castle' made two

55

Top:
'Britannia' Pacific No 70024 *Vulcan* arrives at St David's with the 11.00am Paddington-Plymouth on 25 April 1952. On the left, an 'E1/R' class 0-6-2T on banking duties stands in the headshunt. *T. Reardon*

Above:
'Royal Scot' No 46162, *Queen's Westminster Rifleman*, renumbered but still in LMS livery, with an up express at St David's during the 1948 Locomotive Exchanges. Note the dynamometer car, first vehicle behind the tender.
T. Reardon

return trips to Kingswear. The rest of the shed's duties at that period were mainly local. Various BR standard classes appeared, although they never eclipsed the established classes. Types seen were

'Britannia' Pacifics 9F 2-10-0s, 4-6-0s of Classes 4 & 5, and Class 3 2-6-2Ts, the latter being additional to those at Exmouth Junction.

Several 'foreign' engines have worked through St David's, one of the first being Robinson Great Central Railway Atlantic No 267 which drew an excursion from Manchester to Plymouth in October 1904, while in the 1925 Locomotive Exchange with the LNER, Gresley Pacific No 4474 *Victor Wild* passed through, LMS 4-4-0 compound No 1047 appearing the following year. World War 2 saw the appearance of 2-8-0s of the LMS Class 8 and also the British and American 'Austerity' types. In order to familiarise crews with both roads from Exmouth to Plymouth so that in the event of one being blocked an alternative could be used, SR engines and crews regularly worked the 11.25am St David's-Newton Abbot and the 12.30pm Newton-Plymouth (North Road) returning at 4.30pm; and also the 2.15pm Plymouth (North Road)-Newton and the 4pm Newton-St David's, returning at 5.30pm. With Nationalisation came further locomotive exchanges in 1948, the following working from Paddington-Plymouth via Westbury:

LMR 'Coronation' 4-6-2 No 46236 *City of Bradford*
    'Royal Scot' 4-6-0 No 46162 *Queen's Westminster Rifleman*
ER 'A4' class 4-6-2 No 60022 *Mallard*
                No 60033 *Seagull*
SR 'Merchant Navy' class No 35019 *French Line CGT*

and the following Bristol-Plymouth:

LMR Class 5   4-6-0 No 45253
ER 'B1' Class   4-6-0 No 61251 *Oliver Bury*
SR 'West Country' 4-6-2 No 34006 *Bude*

No 46237 *City of Bristol* appeared in 1955 on dynamometer car trials between Paddington and Plymouth with the 'Cornish Riviera Express', while the following year, failures of welding in 'King' class bogies caused some replacement locomotives to be borrowed from the LMR and 'Duchess' class Nos 46254 *City of Stoke-on-Trent* and 46257 *City of Salford* worked through Exeter on Plymouth turns and 'Princess Royal' class No 46210 *Lady Patricia* also made a trip or two. Class 6 'Clan' pacific No 72005 *Clan Macgregor* worked through on a Bradford-Paignton train on 8 July 1960 and on 15 September 1962 'Jubilee' No 45660 *Rooke* arrived with the 3.33pm Bristol-Penzance parcels train.

From 1958 steam was rapidly displaced from the ex-GWR West of England main line and branches. First came the five North British Locomotive Co A1A-A1A 'Warship' diesel-hydraulics Nos D600-D604. These were soon followed by the much lighter B-B 'Warships' built by Swindon and by NBL (later Classes 42 and 43). For local services NBL supplied the Type 2 B-B diesel-hydraulics (later Class 22) which were essentially a single-engine version of the twin-engine Type 4 'Warships'. In later years the Type 2 'Baby Warships' were confined almost entirely to local freight duties. The Beyer-Peacock Type 3 'Hymeks' also appeared in the area on certain services, though not in very large numbers.

In 1961 there appeared the largest and perhaps most successful diesel-hydraulic design, the 2,700hp 'Western' class of which 74 examples were built. These displaced the 'Warships' on most top express duties and were a central feature of Western Region motive power, on Devon and Cornwall-Paddington services.

By January 1972 the survivors of Class 22 were all withdrawn, replaced by Class 25 and Class 31 locomotives on local duties. By the end of 1972 the 'Warships', were also extinct, largely replaced by members of Class 46 and Class 47. The Class 52 'Westerns' continued in service until February 1977 when the last of the hydraulic designs disappeared, having gradually been supplanted by the 50

Below:
British Railways 204hp 0-6-0 diesel-mechanical shunter No D2131 shunting stock in platform 1 at St David's. These locomotives were later displaced by the standard 350hp 0-6-0 diesel-electric shunter, later classified '08'.
Lens of Sutton

members of Class 50, displaced from their former duties by the West Coast main line electrification to Glasgow.

The Western Region said goodbye to its Class 25 locomotives in 1980, leaving local services in the hands of Classes 31 and 33. Class 46 became extinct in November 1984.

Today on the former Great Western line passenger trains are worked by diesel electrics of Classes 45, 47 and 50, many expresses being HSTs, these starting from Paddington-Penzance in the autumn of 1979. Locomotives of Class 37 appear to some extent on freights and in summer, occasionally on passenger trains. A highly unusual

Below:

Class 52 diesel-hydraulic No 1040 *Western Queen* **leaving St David's with the 12.26 Paddington-Torquay on 16 August 1975.** *Col M. H. Cobb*

Bottom:

Until the introduction of the 'Westerns', the B-B 'Warships' were the prime express motive power in the west country. The first member of the class No D800 *Sir Brian Robertson* **stands at St David's with a down train on 26 July 1960.** *Frank Church*

visitor on 1 September 1984 was No 58.002 hauling a partly failed HST forming the 12.10 Liverpool-Penzance. The Class 58 worked to Plymouth and was towed back light the same day experiencing brake problems on the gradients.

Below:
Successors to the NBL Class 22 locomotives were members of Class 25. No 25.223 climbs the bank out of St David's with a trip freight on 13 July 1976. *Brian Morrison*

Bottom:
Electric train heating fitted Class 45 No 45.109 arrives at Exeter St David's with the 13.40 Paddington-Penzance on 28 August 1984. A very unusual working for a Class 45 locomotive. *Author*

Local services are worked by Classes 31, 33 and DMUs of Classes 117 and 118. The DMUs are based at Laira and go there for maintenance, though they are swept out at Exeter. C&W technicians inspect DMUs at Exeter and change the brake blocks if necessary. Out of the five DMUs at Exeter, three go to Laira empty every night, a distance of 49½ miles, the other two staying at Exeter. They run 550 miles between fuelling. All DMU services in Devon and Cornwall are now second class only, former first class accommodation being de-rated. Thirteen two-car Class 142 DMUs have been authorised for Laira and will be in service from 1986 onwards: six for Exeter, six for Cornwall and one on

Above:

Class 47 No 47.508 *Great Britain* arrives at St David's with a Penzance-Paddington relief service on 28 August 1984. *Author*

Below:

Swindon three-car cross-country DMU set No 552 with a St David's-Exmouth train approaching Exmouth Junction past a fine signal gantry on 29 September 1977. *Col M. H. Cobb*

maintenance turnover. They will run as two-car sets to Exmouth, Barnstaple and Torbay, with four-car sets at peak periods.

Two Class 08 locomotives are scheduled to shunt and work local freight trips in the area, one engine working trips between Riverside marshalling yard and City Basin/Exeter Central/Exmouth Junction and vice versa, working 06.45-16.30 each Monday-Friday, then shunting at St David's station from 16.30-04.30 each Monday-Friday night. It is stabled during Saturday and Sunday except for some parcel/newspaper van shunting at St David's station between 02.30 and 04.00 Sunday morning. The second Class 08 works 00.01-06.00 each Monday morning shunting at St David's passenger station, then working 06.15 Monday until 05.45 Saturday as Exeter Riverside yard pilot.

The relatively severe gradients of 1 in 70 west of Salisbury affected the choice of locomotives over the route, engines with 6ft coupled wheels being used instead of the 6ft 7in wheels as elsewhere on the LSWR system, though at least one competent observer believed that in pre-Bulleid Pacific days the best work between Salisbury and Exeter was always done by 6ft 7in engines rather than those with smaller wheels. By the summer of 1875 the 2-4-0s were finding express work too heavy and in June that year the 2.10pm ex Waterloo arrived punctually on only four occasions, the average time of arrival being 8¾min late. A pilot engine was added to this and several other trains to solve the difficulty. Adams 380 class 4-4-0s appeared in 1880, while in May 1883 following trials with No 135 of the Adams '135' class 6ft 7in 4-4-0s, Nos 141/2/3 were shedded at Exeter for use on the best services to Salisbury, similar engines but with smaller boilers and classed as '460' appearing in 1884. The 'X2' class 4-4-0s Nos 591/5 with 7ft 1in coupled wheels were lent to Exmouth Junction for use on the heaviest expresses and a series of test runs over the line were made during July 1891 with No 582. Its success led to Adams ordering 10 basically similar engines known as the 'T3' class and having longer fireboxes and 6ft 7in coupled wheels replacing the '460' class on the harder runs. They proved successful on express passenger trains and also appeared frequently on local freight trips around Exeter. During World War 1 they were used as pilots on the heavy Salisbury-Exeter expresses and on specials run for the Royal Navy. In 1917 when Plymouth was an important anti-submarine base, a daily explosives train originating from the Thameside ran to Plymouth, 'T3' Nos 558 and 566 handling the train between Salisbury and Plymouth, engines being changed at Exeter.

Below:
Adams '380' class 4-4-0 No 162 on the duplicate list stands at Exmouth Junction coaling stage in LSWR livery on 19 July 1924. *H. C. Casserley*

Drummond 'T9' 4-4-0s introduced in 1899 proved ideal for working the two new steam-heated corridor trains for the West of England expresses, 10 'T9s' being specially equipped with steam heating apparatus. The train sets were put into operation on 1 January 1901 on the 10.50am and 3.0pm down and the 8.20am and 9.55am up expresses. Mixed traffic 'L11' 4-4-0s with 5ft 7in coupled wheels handled semi-fast trains. Great things were expected of Drummond's 'F13' class 4-6-0s, but they proved very sluggish and heavy on coal as were Drummond's subsequent engines of this wheel arrangement and the 'T9' 4-4-0s were preferred. 'H15' and 'S15' mixed traffic 4-6-0s and 'N15' express engines handled trains well, 'King Arthurs' putting in arduous work over the line between Exeter and Salisbury, a pre-1939 rostered duty involving 16hr running and covering 360 miles. With the introduction of Bulleid Pacifics of the 'Merchant Navy', 'Battle of Britain' and 'West Country' classes, these engines took over most of the passenger trains.

Top:
A triple-headed down passenger train at St David's on 24 July 1954, headed by 'T9' No 30727, 'West Country' No 34035 *Shaftesbury* and 'N' class No 31845. *J. H. Bamsey*

Above:
Urie 'King Arthur' class No 744 *Maid of Astolat* at Exmouth Junction shed on 16 September 1936. The lifting bay is to the left of the building. *H. C. Casserley*

Above:
An up triple header arrives at St David's. '700' class 0-6-0 No 30315, 2-6-0 and a Bulleid light Pacific head a Saturday train from Ilfracombe in September 1956. *T. Reardon*

Below:
Maunsell 'N' class 2-6-0 No 31851 with a Plymouth Friary-Exmouth Junction freight leaves platform 3 at St David's at the foot of the incline to Central. *T. Reardon*

In 1951 the nine 'Merchant Navies' shedded at Exmouth Junction worked the principal expresses; 30 'WC' and 'BB' pacifics being employed on other main line work; 17 'N' Class 2-6-0s were used on passenger and goods trains principally over the North Cornwall line to Wadebridge and Padstow, and also Bude; Six 'T9' 4-4-0s ran to Okehampton and Wadebridge. 'S15' 4-6-0s were used on freight working to Salisbury and 3 '0395' 0-6-0s for snowplough duties and emergencies. Twenty-five 'M7' 0-4-4Ts were utilised for duties on the various East Devon branch lines and as Exeter Central pilot, banking and goods trains. Four Stroudley 'E1/R' 0-6-2Ts were used for banking and transfer goods trips, whilst four '02' class 0-4-4Ts were also available if required, this class being the only type of engine allowed on Exmouth Quay and Topsham Quay. Three '0415' class 4-4-2Ts were based at

Above:
'Battle of Britain' light Pacific No 34054 *Lord Beaverbrook* stands at platform 4 with the 10.15am Exeter-Ilfracombe. Note the milk tanks next to the locomotive. 3 May 1964.
 Hugh Ballantyne

Below:
Bulleid 'Merchant Navy' Pacific No 21C4 *Cunard White Star* carrying the 'Devon Belle' headboards at Exmouth Junction on 14 September 1947. *R. C. Riley*

Above:
Rebuilt 'Merchant Navy' No 35018
British India Line **at Central station
on 20 June 1959.** *W. Potter*

Left:
**Near the end of their lives, some of
the Maunsell 'Schools' class worked
on the Waterloo-Exeter line after
displacement from their traditional
duties. No 30913** ***Christ's Hospital***
**passes St James' Park halt with the
1.05pm Waterloo-Exeter Central in
the early 1960s.** *R. A. Lumber*

Below left:
**'700' class No 30689 with large
snowplough attached to the
bufferbeam stands in steam at
Exmouth Junction on 16 February
1963.** *R. A. Lumber*

Exmouth Junction, one being sent weekly to the Lyme Regis branch. 'Z' class 0-8-0T No 30954 nicknamed 'Dolly' shunted Exmouth Junction yard from Tuesday till Saturday, the yard being closed on Sunday . On Monday an 'E1/R' relieved 'Dolly ' while she had a boiler washout. Latterly others of the 'Z' class were allocated to Exmouth Junction to provide improved banking power. Around 1960 4-4-0 'Schools' class often came down to Exeter and during World War 2 a few USA Class S160 2-8-0s were allocated to Exmouth Junction.

Below:
No 30374, one of the Drummond 'M7' tanks with sandboxes fitted beneath the footplate stands in platform 3 at St David's with a freight train on 28 July 1949. *W. Potter*

Bottom:
'Z' class 0-8-0T No 30954 at Exmouth Junction on 8 July 1949, still carrying the word 'Southern' on its tank sides. *H. C. Casserley*

In 1948 following the Locomotive Exchanges on the WR, a similar series of trials took place between Waterloo and Exeter. The visitors were Nos 46236, 60022 and 60033 as on the WR, and 'Royal Scot' No 46154 *The Hussar*. Only express passenger classes were involved.

As No 35020 *Bibby Line* was descending Crewkerne bank at speed on 24 April 1953 the axle on the middle pair of driving wheels broke. This resulted in all Bulleid Pacifics being withdrawn for checking and were temporarily replaced by

engines lent by other regions. The following unusual locomotives are also on record:

23 August 1962 Q1 No 33021 on the 4.40am Southampton Downs-Riverside banana special;
18 December 1962 USA 0-6-0T No DS234 at Exeter Junction;
2 May 1964 No 4707 on Westbury-Exeter Central (via Taunton) cement train.

'Lion' class 0-6-0 goods engines No 65 *Achilles*, No 111 *Test* and 113 *Stour* were shedded at Exeter in the early 1870s, though No 16 *Salisbury* of Yeovil shed was invariably rostered on the 9.40am semi-fast passenger to Exeter, working back on the 4.20pm. Nos 241/2, Beattie's double framed Beyer Peacock 0-6-0s were shedded at Exeter in 1867. Seven years later, three similar, but more modern single frame locomotives Nos 308/10/11 were allocated to Exeter, though they proved themselves less successful than their older sisters, so much so that Salisbury crews refused to work the 'Tavy' and all other heavy goods over the Exeter road with a single framed engine. In 1861 the little 'Nelson' 2-4-0WT No 144 *Howe* worked the Exmouth branch and was also employed on other passenger and freight duties from Exeter. On 17 May 1862 while working the 4.20pm up from Crediton, it left the road at Cowley Bridge Junction. By 1867 all three members of the class were at Exeter, one usually employed on banking duties from St David's. Drivers preferred 'A12' 0-4-2 'Jubilees' to Adams 0-6-0s for Exeter-Salisbury freights unless the load was greater than 40 wagons when the six-coupled engines came into their own.

In the summer of 1925 'N' class 2-6-0s were first used on the Ilfracombe branch. Locomotives of the 'King Arthur' and 'Lord Nelson' classes were too heavy for the line, but 'West Country' and 'Battle of Britain' lightweight pacifics were within the weight limitations and appeared on many trains.

The Exmouth branch was worked by a wide range of engines, mostly of the tank variety. First were the 2-2-2WTs, 2-4-0WTs, 'Ilfracombe Goods' 0-6-0s appearing in 1881, taking over from Beyer Peacock double frame 0-6-0 No 0288, while the Adams 'G6' 0-6-0Ts shedded at Exmouth Junction for shunting and banking duties, worked goods trains to Exmouth, as did ex-LBSCR 'Terrier' 0-6-0T No 735 which had been found unsuited to the Lyme Regis branch. Adams '415' class 4-4-2Ts worked to Exmouth in the 1880s. 'O2' and later 'M7' 0-4-4Ts were the mainstay of the branch until 1952 when 2-6-2Ts appeared of Ivatt Class 2 and BR Standard Class 3 varieties. Drummond 'H13' class steam railcars Nos 5 and 6 were used for the service which began between Exeter and Topsham on 1 June 1908 and also on the Exeter-Honiton service begun on the previous 26 January, but when the cars were scrapped, motor trains replaced them.

Six new 'Metropolitan', or 'Plymouth' 4-4-0Ts were sent to Exmouth Junction ready for the opening of the road to Plymouth and preparatory

Below:
Another locomotive on loan was LMS Class 5 No 45350, here leaving Central with the 10.17am to Waterloo on 26 May 1953. *J. H. Bamsey*

to this were employed on a variety of passenger and goods turns. Their riding qualities on the Plymouth road were so dangerous that they had to be withdrawn and set to work on slower duties in the London area, though in 1879 Nos 320/2 were returned to Exeter for banking duties.

A couple of 0-4-4Ts were concerned in a comedy of errors between St David's and Queen Street on 15 November 1890. No 241 stopped at St David's station at 9.12pm with an up ballast special consisting of 14 wagons with a brake van at either end. The regular banking engine had just become derailed so No 223 was hastily summoned, but in the darkness, rain and general confusion the fireman of No 223 forgot to couple to the rear brake van so when the train moved off, contact was lost. Instead of wisely keeping well clear, Driver Clarkson on No 223 attempted to buffer up, an almost impossible task under such conditions. To avoid too strong a bump, Clarkson had sent his fireman along the running plate to the smokebox door to act as lookout, this action proving successful. Unfortunately Clarkson in an attempt to gain maximum visibility leaned out too far, struck

his head on the wall of St David's tunnel and was knocked unconscious. In due course the train topped the bank and ran into Queen Street with the unattended engine merrily puffing away at the rear. The two guards and crew of No 241 attempted to bring the train to a halt but failed to do so until No 223's fireman regained the footplate and closed the regulator. The following month's working timetables bore the following notice: 'An engineman and his fireman have been fined £3 each for improper and careless banking between St David's and Queen Street stations, Exeter.'

In 1940 LBSCR 'D3' class 0-4-4Ts Nos 2372/3/84/5 were temporarily stored in the carriage shed at Exeter Central as part of a dispersal policy as were 'D1' 0-4-2Ts Nos 2358 and 2699. The earliest 'foreign' engine to work over the line was Webb's LNWR three-cylinder compound No 300 Com-

Right:
The most unusual locomotive called upon to deputise for the 'Merchant Navy' class were members of Gresley's 2-6-2 'V2' class. Here No 60928 is seen at Exmouth Junction, having arrived off the 11.00am Waterloo-Sidmouth on 23 May 1953. *J. H. Bamsey*

Below:
Standard 2-6-2T No 82013 pilots a WR 2-6-0 arriving at St David's with an up Southern Region train, running into the platform 3 road. *T. Reardon*

pound which in May 1884 was tested between Waterloo and Exeter. It coped climbing the banks, but was not free running enough to speed down the other side and therefore lost time, also consuming more coal and water than did the Adams 4-4-0s.

Most passenger trains changed engines at Central, in 1952 the only exceptions being the 5.58am ex Plymouth Friary which worked through to Salisbury, the 8.53am ex Torrington which changed the engines at Yeovil Junction and the 11am Plymouth-Brighton which also worked through to Salisbury. In the down direction were the 11.30am Brighton-Plymouth and the 6.20am and 7.40am ex Yeovil Town whose engines worked through to Plymouth.

SR diesel-electric locomotives Nos 10201/2/3 appeared on Waterloo-Exeter trains in the early 1950s and use was maximised by one coming down on the 1.25am ex Waterloo, returning on the 7.30am from Exeter, going west again on the 1pm from Waterloo and returning from Exeter at 5.55pm, keeping up a daily mileage of 687 miles on six days a week. Later, LMR diesels Nos 10000/1 also appeared.

Western Region 'Warship' diesel-hydraulic locomotives replaced steam locomotives on Exeter-Waterloo expresses, the timetable being re-patterned to enable most through trains to stop at all the remaining stations without too much sacrifice of overall time. From 4 October 1971 trains were hauled by the less powerful SR Class 33 diesel-electrics. 12 May 1980 saw the introduction of 2,700hp Class 50 locomotives which chopped 12min off the Salisbury-Exeter run. Although Class 50s were normally rostered for Waterloo-Exeter trains, in 1984 a Class 47 was booked for the 01.45 ex Waterloo newspaper and passenger train and the 06.45 return to Waterloo, while the 16.38 from Waterloo and 21.00 from Exeter were Class 33 hauled. Class 201 Hastings DEMUs first used the line on a through Saturdays only Brighton-Exeter running throughout the year starting on 6 May 1972 and continuing until 30 April 1977 when it reverted to locomotive haulage, often being worked by pairs of Class 33s. A most unusual occurrence was the appearance of electro-diesel No 73.103 leading a test train on 14 May 1981.

Had the Southern Region kept control of the Salisbury-Exeter line it might well have been electrified, as when Buckhorn Weston Tunnel was relined in 1958, provision was made to lower the track formation to allow for overhead electrification and a projection that year foresaw 1973 as the date of electrification, preceded by diesel traction in 1962.

Below:
Last day of the Hastings DEMU sets at Exeter Central. Units Nos 1033 & 1034 form the 13.55 St David's-Brighton on Saturday 30 April 1977. *R. A. Lumber*

Exeter Gaslight & Coke Company's works were served by the City Basin branch line opened in 1867 to serve the Exeter Canal. The private sidings were worked by the company's standard gauge locomotives. Stock consisted of:

Above:

Peckett 0-4-0ST No 2074 stands outside its shed at Exeter gasworks in July 1961. *R. C. Riley*

Number	Name	Wheel arrangement	Builder	Works No	Date of building	Date of disposal
		0-4-0ST	Hawthorn, Leslie(?)			pre-5/1905
		0-4-0ST	Peckett	1301	1912	1947
		0-4-0ST	Barclay	737	1893	1942
1	Loco	0-4-0ST	Peckett	2031	1942	1956*
2	Loco	0-4-0ST	Peckett	2074	1946	1965
3		0-4-0DH	Hunslet	6263	1964	1971
		4 wheel diesel mechanical	Ruston & Hornsby	402809	1956	1971

* to Dart Valley Railway Co Ltd 9/1969

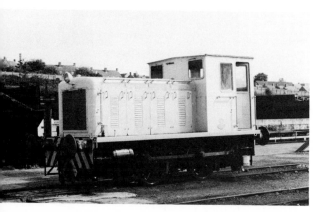

Renwick, Wilton & Dobson (Fuels) Ltd, now Western Fuels Limited, opened a coal concentration depot at Exmouth Junction on the site of ths SR Engineer's Department Concrete Works in 1967. The standard gauge sidings are worked by a diesel-mechanical 0-4-0 ex W. Cory & Sons Ltd, Gallions Jetty, Essex. Built in 1949 it is Drewry Car Co Ltd works No 2269 and Vulcan Foundry No D98.

Left:

Drewry 0-4-0DM No 2269 at Exmouth Junction coal concentration yard on 7 August 1984. *Author*

Motive Power Depots

Between 1844 and 1851 the B&E used a small temporary locomotive shed but that year a new building opened between the down passenger platform and the river. Measuring 150ft by 50ft it was probably constructed of timber. It had three straight roads and accommodated at least 15 engines. A coke plant was situated to the east, early engines burning this fuel in order to avoid smoke problems. The shed closed about 1864 during the station's rebuilding. It is recorded that the old shed was 'to be converted into a dwelling house for the foreman of the new shed'.

The single road SDR shed was built in line with the down station building and situated at its southern end. Opened in July 1846 it measured 100ft by 20ft and was probably built of stone; like its B&E counterpart, it closed about 1864 during the station rebuilding and was converted into a carriage shed. The B&E and SDR loco sheds were replaced by a new depot at the opposite end of the B&E loco yard, the building measuring 135ft by 70ft. In 1894 the shed was extended and a coaling stage with ramp approach added. The water tank was situated above the pump house and therefore could not form the coaling stage roof as was often the practice. The coaling stage was roofed with slate. In 1913 the yard and shed layout were further improved during alterations to the station and goods yard. The brick built shed finally measured 195ft by 70ft, had four straight roads in addition to that through the lifting shop. Its GWR code was EXE, and later British Railways, Western Region 83C. It closed to steam on 14 October 1963, the allocation being divided between Taunton, Plymouth Laira, Yeovil Town, Gloucester Barnwood and Oxford. Its site is now used as a small diesel maintenance depot for Class 08 shunters and Civil Engineering Department machines, larger locomotives also being fuelled and receiving minor attention. The number of engines seen there today varies – at times there may be as many as a dozen and at others none at all. In 1907 the shed had about 200 enginemen, fitters and cleaners.

Whenever the turntable at either of the sheds was out of action, engines were turned on the table at the other shed. The WR usually re-diagrammed locomotive workings to make greater use of tank engines on local trains so that the number requiring turning was reduced to a minimum. This was not possible on the SR and on such occasions groups of locomotives came to St David's to be turned.

Below:
St David's shed on 25 May 1929. Visible from left to right are 0-6-0PTs Nos 1753 & 1617, 'Star' class 4-6-0 No 4032 *Queen Alexandra*, former Cambrian Railways small 2-4-0T No 1192 and Churchward 2-6-0 No 8344. *H. C. Casserley*

Top:
St David's shed on 1 September 1955. From left to right are ex-War Department 2-8-0 No 90563, 'Castle' class No 5021 *Whittington Castle* and 2-6-0 No 6360. The traditional-design coaling stage is clearly visible.   *W. Potter*

Centre:
A solitary Class 08 shunter in the roofless remains of the engine shed at St David's on 16 August 1975. To the left of

the '08' is the train heating van.   *Col. M. H. Cobb*

Bottom:
The old Exmouth Junction shed c1926. Visible are 'N' class 2-6-0 No A852, unsuperheated 'T9' class 4-4-0 No E717 and '0395' class 0-6-0 No 83 on the duplicate list.
Real Photographs

The first LSWR shed at Exeter was a straight three-road depot situated to the east of Queen Street station on the down side of the line. When a shed opened at Exmouth Junction in 1880, the old shed continued to be used for servicing locomotives and although the buildings had been demolished by 1904, the turntable and coal stage were not finally removed until the station re-modelling in 1930. The new shed at Exmouth Junction was a steel framed structure clad in corrugated iron. Measuring 225ft by 165ft it had 11 through roads with accommodation for 40 engines. A ramped coal stage was to the north and coal stack to the north west, while a turntable, latterly 65ft, stood to the east. One of the principal sheds on the LSWR, apart from providing motive power for main line and local trains, it was also responsible for locomotives at the many sub sheds in Devon and Cornwall: Callington, Bude, Exmouth, Launceston, Lyme Regis, Okehampton, Seaton and Sidmouth. The shed fell into disrepair during World War 1 and in 1922 the decision was taken to rebuild in ferro-concrete. Although work began in 1923, it was not completed until 1928 as the scheme included reconstructing the concrete works and rolling stock depots in addition to the running shed. It was built slightly to the east of the 1880 depot and instead of having a yard both ends, was single ended. Measuring 270ft by 249ft it had 12 roads, each with a pit running its whole length and one serving the repair shed which had a much more lofty roof. The repair shed contained the lifting bay which ran the whole length of the

building and was equipped with a 50ton electric overhead travelling gantry crane supplied by Herbert Morris Ltd, of Loughborough. On the north side of this road No 13 were the offices and shops, the latter comprising a fully equipped fitters' shop, machine shop, smiths' shop and store. Slotting, shaping, planing and drilling machines were installed, also axlebox and other lathes. A hydraulic press dealt with coupling rod bushes. The various machines derived their power from two lines of shafting driven by a 30hp electric motor though the wheel lathe in the lifting shop was worked by a 20hp motor. Current for electric lighting and power was brought in from the Exeter City Corporation supply, two special triangular towers of bonded ferro-concrete being used to carry the overhead wires across the main line. Current was taken at a voltage of 2,000v and transformed down to 200v, for lighting and 600v for power. A narrow gauge plateway was laid around part of the shed's exterior to accommodate hand-propelled flats transporting materials and stores.

Smoke vents constructed of concrete ran the length of each shed road and were provided with special channels along the inside of the bottom edge to collect any moisture condensing on the inside, such precipitation being discharged clear of the tracks by gargoyles set at intervals. The roof was supported on concrete columns 1ft square and approximately 18ft high. The base of each column was carried on a specially designed concrete raft in order to distribute the load and necessary because the shed stood on an embankment formed about

Above:
The old shed at Exmouth Junction looks rather dilapidated in this view on 18 July 1925. From left to right: 'G6' class 0-6-0T No 272, '0415' class 4-4-42T No 59 and '02' class 0-4-4T No 228, representatives of three useful Adams classes. *H. C. Casserley*

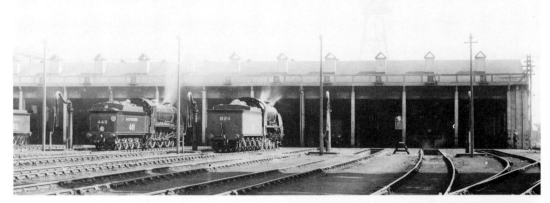

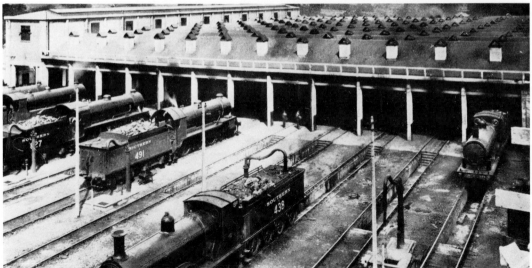

1860. The contractors for the construction of the shed were A. Jackaman & Son Ltd of Slough. During rebuilding, the 65ft turntable was moved slightly southwards and electrically operated, while in 1947 it was replaced by a 70ft table operated by a vacuum worked motor. One of the features of the 1929 shed was the ferro-concrete coaling plant constructed by the Mitchell Conveyor Company, the bunker containing 300tons of coal and capable of coaling two locomotives simultaneously. When the plant began to receive the very friable South Wales coal, complaints were received from householders on the Stoke Hill estate as this coal produced clouds of fine dust when tippled into the hopper at a height of 60ft. The trouble was obviated by fitting a hood. The depot's water tank was situated high on a tower. All water collected in the pits as a result of washing locomotives was passed through a purifying and filtering plant before being pumped to the water tower for re-use, the height of the tower ensuring the necessary pressure for spraying purposes. Although the company bought its water from the corporation at a specially low rate, the need for economy was so imperative that the cost was brought down by re-cycling. The water tank structure incorporated a semaphore signal for eyesight tests. During World War 2 the depot was machine-gunned by a German plane. In 1946-47 oil tanks were provided to refill steam engines converted to oil firing, but with the shortage of foreign currency to buy the oil, soon the project had to be abandoned. Only one oil burning engine actually operated from Exmouth Junction, 'U' class No 1625 and oil-pump locomotive No 701S of the 'D1' class was utilised, but had the scheme fully materialised this would

have been replaced by permanent boilers. The shed had a 45ton breakdown crane No 1580S. Exmouth Junction was rated one of the SR's premier depots and was under the control of a Locomotive Running Shed Superintendent rather than a locomotive foreman as were the moderately important depots. In 1926 the shed employed 430 men, this figure including 119 pairs of drivers/firemen.

During the post World War 2 era, Bulleid was able to introduce the French TIA system of briquettes putting various chemical compositions into canisters placed in locomotive tanks, this neutralising the corrosive constituents of the feedwater to near zero and allowing the period between washouts at Exmouth Junction to be prolonged on several classes of engine to as much as 56 working days. The depot closed to steam in 1965, continuing to service diesels until 6 March 1967. The turntable was removed in 1966 and the buildings and coaling plant demolished in 1970. Royal Marines attempted to blow up the hopper but failed and it had to be knocked down piecemeal. Leo's Co-op supermarket has been built on the site. Exmouth Junction received the British Railways code 72A and was re-coded 83D in December 1962 when transferred to the Western Region.

Below left:
'U' class 2-6-0 No 1625 converted for oil burning leaves St David's for Central with a Plymouth-Waterloo train on a very wet 17 January 1948. *T. Reardon*

Below:
Exmouth Junction water tower with signal for sight tests c1951. *M. E. J. Deane*

Passenger Stations, Goods Sheds and other Depots

The city council refused to let the B&E build a station within the city or allow the railway to run through any part of it. St David's station, its nomenclature in deference to the parish in which it is situated, stood to the west of the city at Red Cow village and therefore lent itself to Brunel's one-sided pattern, with up and down platforms both on the city side of the line and obviating the need for passengers and luggage to cross the running lines. The up platform was to the north and the down to the south. Built by Messrs Hooper of Exeter as were all the buildings in the complex, the departure station was a parallelogram 144ft in length covered with a slate and zinc roof of 40ft span. To the south and in line with this building, were two carriage sheds each about 100ft in length, with plank roofs covered with tarpaulin, a carriage turntable separating the two sheds. The arrival station was similar to that for departure, but with not so many rooms. Water for the station was supplied by the Exeter Water Company, while light was provided by the Exeter Gas Company. With the opening of the SDR, the B&E leased accommodation to the SDR for a yearly rental of £1,300. Although the new station was not completed until 1864, the B&E increased the rent to £3,500 in 1862. Two stationmasters reigned at St David's in 1850, Robert Ashbee representing the B&E and Thomas Batt the SDR. Outside the station was a ticket platform situated north of the later Exeter East signalbox causing an extra stop for passenger trains and was a nuisance tolerated with the early 'open station' concept.

The rather inconvenient one-sided station would have been quite unable to cope with LSWR traffic in addition to that of the B&E and SDR, so following negotiations with the LSWR in 1859 for the erection of a new station, an Act was obtained in March 1860. The station was designed jointly by Francis Fox, the B&E engineer and a pupil of Brunel who designed the roof, and Henry Lloyd, a Bristol architect responsible for the buildings. The work cost £48,203 made up of £29,763 for the new passenger station (the masonry, carpentry, glazing and decorations amounting to about £18,000 and ironwork £9,000), £1,437 for narrow gauge rail, the balance being for the demolition and removal of the old station, and the building of goods sidings, engine sheds and minor works. The LSWR paid the B&E for transhipment of goods between the gauges plus a 60% mileage proportion for running over the line to Cowley Bridge Junction.

Messrs Spiller & Son of Taunton won the building contract, Kerslake of Exeter supplying the 300ton of ironwork for the roof, the 25 wrought iron principals weighing about 60ton. The 30ton of rolled plate glass were supplied by the St Helen's Company, Liverpool. The station, 360ft in length, was faced with Westleigh stone; the cornices, parapets, dressings and arches being in Bath freestone. The facade rising above the offices and facing the approach road was divided into three bays having parapets surmounted by 26 massive classical ornamental urns. The roof ridge was 60ft high with a continuous skylight extending about 12ft down each side of the ridge, the rest being

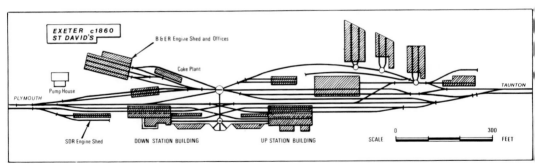

SDR Engine Shed   DOWN STATION BUILDING   UP STATION BUILDING   SCALE

Below:
The east end of St David's station c1905.
Devon Library Services

Bottom:
The road frontage to St David's station c1905.
Lens of Sutton

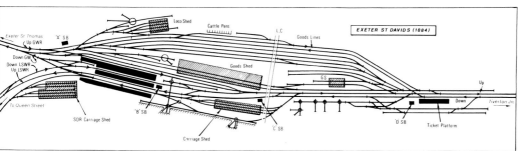

slate covered. The roof itself was 132ft wide by 363ft long. It was constructed of 23 wrought iron trusses of the Fink type, spaced 15ft apart, bearing on masonry walls 32ft high. Because of the roof's elevation, weather screens of glazed ornamental ironwork were erected at both ends and supported on cast iron columns. A double row of windows on the up side made the interior of the train shed unusually light, while at night a triple row of incandescent gas lamps provided illumination.

The GWR down platform was 640ft in length; the central island of 510ft was for the use of up and down LSWR trains, while the western island platform 750ft long was for LSWR down and GWR up trains. There was only one road between the two island platforms which restricted their operational value. A trelliswork luggage bridge was built to the north of the passenger footbridge, baggage being raised by hydraulic lifts. Towards the end of the broad gauge era a considerable transfer of traffic took place at St David's, all narrow gauge trains from the north via the Severn Tunnel terminating at the station and traffic having to be transferred to the broad gauge. St David's had become the busiest railway station in the West Country, a title it has kept to the present day.

Exeter St David's statistics

Date	Passengers	Passenger Receipts	Parcels Forward	Received	Horses & dogs Forward	Received
Jan 1895	12,574	£2,955	4,340	2,858	378	1,342
Jly 1895	22,077	£4,311	4,813	3,196	539	2,734
Jly 1914	28,755	£7,227	9,217	9,100	1,354	2,339
Jly 1939	22,021	£9,080	5,679	17,000	575	3,134

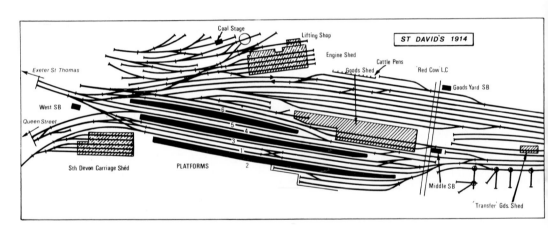

The St David's staff in 1891 consisted of: 1 stationmaster; 5 clerks; 3 inspectors; 8 passenger guards; 24 goods guards; 23 police/signalmen and ticket collectors; 31 porters & 14 supernumery; 3 lampmen.

Further improvements to the station were planned in 1908 and although some work was carried out the following year, it was 1912 before work started in earnest. The new layout followed the plan of that displaced, but provided two additional running lines through the station, ie an additional through line between the down and middle platform available for trains of either company not requiring to call at a platform and an additional platform road between the middle and up platforms forming part of the GWR main line.

Preliminary work consisted of removing the island platforms and rebuilding them on new sites. Temporary structures containing refreshment, waiting and lavatory accommodation were provided during the alterations and since they were constructed of timber and portable, could be transferred to different positions as the building worked progressed.

Early in the spring of 1912 a contract was let to Messrs C. H. Hunt & Sons, High Wycombe, for the removal of the train shed roof and the erection of new platform coverings, new station buildings, a new passenger footbridge and a new luggage footbridge, work commencing in April. In order to dismantle the train shed roof, a travelling gantry was used, extending 130ft between the station walls and having a deck 30ft wide at a height of 34ft above the rails. It was carried on wheels set on the up main and down through roads, the latter having to be slewed parallel for the purpose. It was found possible to dismantle 3 trusses carrying 7,000 sq ft of roof within a week.

'As it was undesirable to have the platforms denuded of covering at any time, it was stipulated in the contract that after a certain extent of the existing roof had been removed, the process of demolition should be stayed until the platforms which had become exposed to the weather had been re-covered by the erection of the new verandahs.

'In the case of the Down platform, a temporary covering had to be provided before any portion of the old roof was removed. This was necessary owing to the extensive use of this platform by the public and the station staff. In the case of the Down and Middle platform a certain amount of preliminary work in provision of foundations and erection of CI standards for supporting the roof could be carried forward independently of the roof demolition, and this was taken in hand early in the contract.

Below:
Erecting a new platform canopy within the train shed at St David's, 1912. *BR/OPC*

Bottom:
An up view at St David's c1914. *Locomotive Publishing Co*

'The new coverings on the island platforms are of the standard Great Western type. The superstructure is carried entirely by a double row of CI columns on the Middle platform, whereas on the Up platform the support is given partly by columns and partly by new buildings. They are intersected by the new footbridge* covering near the mid-point of their length and are terminated at their northern extremity by the new luggage bridge. The superstructure consists of No 12 lattice cantilever principals, 30ft centre to centre, linked by a double system of longitudinal stiffening trusses running throughout the length. The trusses carry intermediate cantilever principals at their mid-span, thus reducing the span length of the purlins and valance plates to 15ft. The coverings consist approximately of equal areas of glazing and patent galvanised sheeting.

'The new roof on the Down platform is of special design. It consists of two distinct coverings of about equal areas erected at different levels, the "upper" having its supports at practically the same level as the old roof, and the "lower", a cantilever roof, carried at the same height as those erected on the island platform. The space between the upper and lower coverings is closed by a vertical screen consisting of muffled plate-glass set in ornamental iron frames of the Fenestra type.

'The chief factor governing the design is found in the existence of the main frontal wall which formed the support for the old station roof. The removal of the wall, a handsome architectural feature forming one side of the office buildings, was not necessitated by the alterations in contemplation, and the adaptation to it of the type of covering described may be regarded as a happy conception resulting not only in the preservation of the architectural features of the station frontal, but incidentally adding pleasing characteristics to the station construction as a whole.'

F.J. Tyley, *Great Western Railway Magazine,* 1915.

Certain additions were made to the buildings adjacent to the down platform and the old architecture copied in new work, the rock-faced quoins and pilasters being formed of light brown oolite of Nailsworth stone and the panel walls coursed rubble, hammer dressed, cut from Westleigh quarries. New buildings on the up platform were entirely of Nailsworth stone on a plinth of Cornish granite, standing 1ft 3in above platform level and on foundations carried down to solid ground found at an average depth of 12ft below the platform.

'The walls are of plain ashlar divided into panels by plain pilasters and decorated with moulded strings and massively-formed cornices. Circular and elliptical arches formed with voussoirs of the same stone, carrying label courses and moulded edges, support the super-incumbent masonry over the doorways and the generously-proportioned window openings.

'The refreshment buildings contain a refreshment room, tea room, kitchen and cellar. The latter has been formed in water-bearing strata the floor of which, during rainy seasons, is well below flood level in the river Exe nearby. Extra precautions had, therefore, to be taken to render the floor and walls impermeable to water. To this end the external surfaces of the walls were coated with bituminous asphalt, and outside this a thick layer of well-puddled clay was deposited. Special drainage

*At one end the passenger footbridge incorporated a direct entrance to the streets via steps and used at busy periods by passengers from platforms 3 to 6. Last used in the 1960s it is now blocked. CGM

Below :
View across St David's footbridge, 28 August 1984. *Author*

arrangements had also to be provided for carrying off the water used in cleansing the cellar.'

ibidem

A considerable proportion of the old footbridge was able to be re-used, the stairs and landings on the down platform not even interfered with. The structure was covered with patent glazing, since removed. Luggage transfer between platforms was improved by hydraulic lifts being replaced by 30cwt electrically operated lifts supplied by the Easton Lift Company working in substantial

masonry towers erected on each platform. The new works were finished early in 1914, but the following year the up and middle platforms had to be lengthened. Displayed on Platform 5 is a copy of the Roll of Honour listing all GWR servants who gave their lives during the 1914-18 War. One disadvantage of the site of St David's was that nearly all shunting movements at the down end required the occupation of the up or down main line where it crossed the River Exe south of the station.

In the autumn of 1938 further improvements were made at St David's, remodelling the building on the down side making it 11ft wider for a distance of 170ft. A broader station entrance was constructed with a large booking hall, and a new storey for the divisional offices located on the first floor. A 350ft canopy stretched the length of the building. The additions were planned by the GWR architect P. E. Culverhouse to fit in with the existing architectural features and were built of Bath stone to match the old structure. At one time it was contemplated having an independent high level line for SR trains, a bridge carrying the tracks from the Central station over those of the GWR and two new lines carrying SR trains to Cowley Bridge Junction, but shortage of funds prevented this interesting scheme from being adopted. It certainly would have eased the traffic flow as an SR train from Central prevented a movement on the main Paddington-Penzance line, while an SR train arriving at Cowley Bridge Junction blocked both lines of the GWR. Work on the first stage of St David's was completed February 1940, the second stage providing a new parcels office, cloakroom and telegraph office being completed in the autumn. A hostel for refreshment room staff was built at the foot of St David's Hill in 1938. A two storey brick building, each bedroom had a washbasin, whilst a comfortable recreation room was available for staff off duty. At this period Platforms Nos 1 & 2 were mainly used by GWR down trains and the Exe Valley push-pull; Nos 3 & 4 by SR trains and Nos 5 & 6 by GWR up trains,

though these last two also handled some down departures including two for the Teign Valley branch, though most of the Heathfield trains left from No 1.

St David's today has been little altered structurally since 1940 – the GWR roundel still graces the stonework above the main entrance; the waiting room on No 1 platform still keeps its 1930s charm; brown and cream tiles flank the stairway to the footbridge. The only obvious modern touch is a new Portakabin style waiting room on Platforms 3 & 4, and electric lights which replaced the gas variety in 1960. Electrically propelled water bowsers for filling water tanks of coaches terminating at St David's can be seen on Platforms 3 & 4, while on Platform 1 is a tank of replenishment coolant which can sometimes help a failed HST engine to start and so avoid having to take on an assistant locomotive to Plymouth.

Right:
Former hostel for refreshment room girls, standing opposite St David's station. *Author*

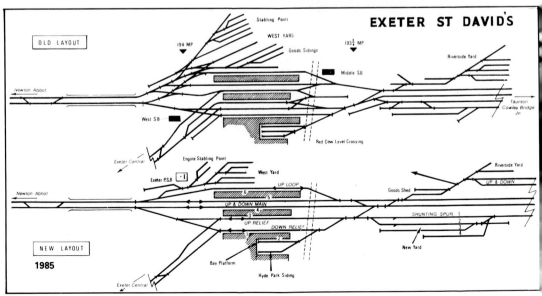

Top left:
Water bowser in use at St David's on 28 August 1984.
Author

Above left:
HST coolant tanks on trolley ready for use, platform 1 St David's on 6 August 1984. *Author*

Top right:
Announcer's cabin on platforms 3/4. Note the attractive cast iron handrail support. 28 August 1984. *Author*

Left:
Alf Edmunds, station announcer, 28 August 1984. *Author*

The announcer's cabin is placed on Platforms 3 & 4. Announcements are read from pre-typed cards, amendments being carried out daily. There are three boxes of cards: weekdays, Saturdays and Sundays. When a train is ready to depart, a Senior Railman on the platform presses a button, this signalling to the announcer that he should ask all passengers to close the doors. Pressing the 'Train Ready to Start' button also informs the signalman that he can clear the signals. The announcer has to record the times of trains entering and leaving in order that any time lost at Exeter can be accounted for, while another task is to relay messages to the Control at Swindon – such as if a train is late, the reason for the delay. He passes information to his colleagues at Plymouth, Newton Abbot, Taunton and Bristol. Exeter Travel Centre passes in outside messages for the announcer and he directs people to the Centre to collect the communication. Railwaymen have taken an important part in local government, at one time the announcer being the Lord Mayor of Exeter.

The open station concept was adopted early in 1982 when station ticket collectors were abolished.

Above:
Class 47 No 47.106 stands at platform 6 Exeter St David's with an up parcels train on 28 August 1984. *Author*

Left:
St David's station ticket office on 6 August 1984. *Author*

Overall savings are marginal because ticket collectors formerly on stations are now on trains. However vandalism in coaches has been reduced as staff patrol while collecting fares, another benefit being that passengers are able to ask the travelling ticket collector questions about travel. St David's issues about ½ million tickets annually,

approximately 1½ million people using it arriving, departing and changing trains.

From the opening of the B&E, five horse omnibuses connected with the arrival and departure of each train, serving Baring Place, Livery Dole, St Thomas Church, Magdalen New Road and Mount Pleasant respectively. From 1 August 1883 the station was served by a horse tramway, it being electrified on 4 April 1905 and closed on 5 August 1931. Today St David's station is served by those country buses routed via Cowley Bridge in addition to a local minibus service.

Below:
Platform indicator switches on platforms 3/4 St David's. 28 August 1984. *Author*

Above:
Mail boxes in office on platform 1, 28 August 1984. *Author*

Left:
Sherborne-Plymouth travelling safe photographed on 28 August 1984. *Author*

Above:
St Thomas station with overall roof. An up view c1920. Note that the up platform is shorter than the down.
Lens of Sutton

Right:
St Thomas down platform.
Lens of Sutton

South of St David's the SDR crossed the River Exe by a timber bridge and when the line was doubled in 1861 it was paralleled by an iron bridge, the present steel structure being erected in 1896.

The original SDR station at St Thomas opened on 30 May 1846 had a single platform and wooden train shed, being the company's headquarters it had an imposing frontage containing offices. When the line from Exeter to Dawlish was doubled in 1861 the opportunity was taken to improve the station and enlarge it. It was renamed St Thomas (Exeter) in April 1853 and Exeter (St Thomas) May 1897. Nine-tenths of the SDR's local traffic from Exeter used St Thomas station as it was more convenient to the commercial centre and fares were lower. It had an overall roof, the skeleton of which lasted until 1971, the glass being taken out in the 1950s. At one time the platforms were partly staggered, but today are opposite one another. In 1930 the down platform was lengthened at the St

David's end, from 400ft to 620ft. As a wartime economy measure St Thomas was closed on 2 April 1917 but re-opened by Sir Robert Newman, MP on 3 March 1919. Closure of the station proved inconvenient to St Thomas residents as it involved a change of tramcar to reach St David's. The station was partially unstaffed on 3 May 1971 and at the time of writing it can be staffed on, for example, a summer Sunday when, if the weather is fine, hundreds of passengers arrive. Today the station is only a shadow of its former self. The station building and arches have been used for commercial purposes since 1959 and the interior steps to the down platform are very shabby. A new exterior staircase has been made to give access to

Left:
St Thomas station east frontage viewed on 6 August 1984. *Author*

Centre:
A Class 52 'Western' diesel-hydraulic passing St Thomas with an up express in June 1976. *Col M. H. Cobb*

Bottom:
A down view of St Thomas on 6 August 1984. Note the new platform shelters. *Author*

the up platform. Although the station suffers from vandals, they do not cause so much trouble here as at other Exeter stations, the policy being that the less there is at an unmanned halt, the less there is to interest mischiefmakers. In 1906 the station staff consisted of a stationmaster, four signalmen and eight porters.

Alphington Halt on the Teign Valley line opened 2 April 1928 having a timber platform and corrugated iron waiting shed with a flat roof. It closed to passengers 9 June 1958.

Queen Street station was built in the Longbrook Valley in a portion of the moat of Rougemont Castle, its piers going down 30ft. The two storeyed domestic style station buildings were of wood with a low pantiled roof. Originally it had only one platform and a bay road, both on the city side of the line. The platform was spanned by a two road train shed. All up trains from the North Devon lines arrived on No 3 road and dropped across the down main to a siding at the west end of the station and so up No 1 or down main line for station work, leaving for London from the No 1 down main. Down trains stopped at the ticket platform immediately east of the Howell Road overbridge before drawing into the main platform. In 1883 the time allowance for inspection was one minute, but the usual time taken was four minutes. Tickets of up trains were collected at the last stopping place before arrival at Exeter, principally Crediton or Newton St Cyres. An up platform and up bay were constructed in 1874 and two more lines through the station spanned by a second roof of wrought iron trusses supported on cast iron columns. There was separate road access to the up and down

Top:
The 12.40pm Newton Abbot-Exeter arriving at Alphington halt behind '1400' class 0-4-2T No 1469 on 1 February 1958. *T. Reardon*

Above:
Alphington halt. *Lens of Sutton*

station buildings. W. Hinde writing in the *Southern Railway Magazine* of December 1933 said that from 1879 until the time he left in 1896 'to keep the old building on the down side together one or two carpenters were employed almost daily to repair the rotten state which presented itself. I have often said I believe I saw the down side rebuilt with wood'. The LSWR directors were not encouraged to rebuild the station because of the fact that it was scheduled as a 'shed' and consequently not rated so heavily as would otherwise have been the case. On 3 June 1927 a fire was discovered just before 10am in the block of waiting rooms, refreshment

An up view of Queen Street station LSWR in 1911. *Lens of Sutton*

Compared with the view in chapter one, the up platform has been lengthened and a scissors crossover inserted. *Lens of Sutton*

rooms and offices which fronted the main approach on the down side. Despite the efforts of the station staff and the city fire brigade, a large portion of the timber built block ignited. After an hour the blaze was put out, but not before causing £2,000 of damage.

The train shed had a gloomy interior not in keeping with a modern image and the announcement of the station's rebuilding was first made by the SR in April 1925, though it was a relatively simple scheme estimated to cost £40,000 and involved lengthening the up main platform by 600ft to the exceptional length of 1,210ft. The two centre roads were kept for light engine movements and station shunting of which there was a great deal as Exeter was the terminus of many restaurant car services and the dividing point for Plymouth, North Devon and North Cornwall portions of West of England trains. The up platform road was connected to the up through road by a scissors

Below:
'King Arthur' class 4-6-0 No 749 *Iseult* **heads an up train on 3 August 1928.** *H. C. Casserley*

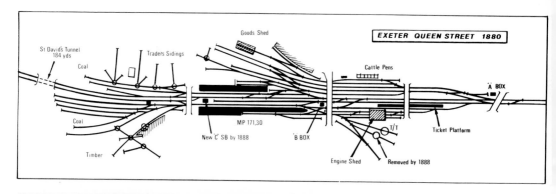

EXETER QUEEN STREET 1880

St David's Tunnel 184 yds

Coal

Coal

Timber

Traders Sidings

Goods Shed

MP 171,30

New 'C' SB by 1888

Cattle Pens

'B BOX

Engine Shed   Removed by 1888

'A' BOX

Ticket Platform

T/T

Above:
A view towards New North Road bridge and Queen Street station. Note the signals on left. *Lens of Sutton*

Left:
'G6' class 0-6-0T No 257 and superheated 'S11' No 401 ascending the last yards into Queen Street on 18 June 1926. Note the 20 mile/hr sign for the descent. Carriage sidings situated on left. *H.C. Casserley*

crossing midway along its length to permit the uniting of the Plymouth and North Devon portions of expresses. One portion of the train was drawn up or propelled to the east end of the platform, whilst the other arrived at the west end. After the second locomotive had been detached and run over the crossover to the centre road, the first portion reversed, buffered up to the second and after coupling was ready to proceed. On summer Saturdays traffic to and from various resorts was sufficiently heavy for through trains to be run,

obviating shunting movements. The length of the up bay was increased by 300ft, but these improvements did not materially alter the station's structure. In February 1930 Exmouth trains started from the up, instead of the down platform bay. From 1933 branch trains used either bay or occasionally Platform 2. In more recent years they have departed from Platforms 1 or 2, or 3 if from St David's, but from 1985 can use No 2 coming from St David's as the down line is reversible between the two stations.

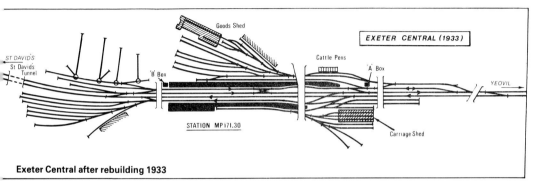

STATION MP 171.30

Exeter Central after rebuilding 1933

Plans by Scott had not been finalised by March 1931 when the scheme estimated to cost £50,000-£60,000 with a two-storey structure had been whittled down to a more economic £35,000 single-storey building as the company was afraid it would not get sufficient tenants for a larger building. The planned New North Road entrance had been abandoned and the sole entrance was to be in Queen Street. The City Council on inspecting the plans believed that a single-storey building opposite the Rougemont Hotel, the tallest secular building in Exeter, would look mean and asked the SR directors to reconsider. Exeter was rather

mortified, too, by the fact that plans for the new station were similar to that at Exmouth. The directors on re-thinking decided on May 1931 to erect a three-storey building in red brick and reinforced concrete with trains in the basement and a two-storeyed crescent above, 259ft in length, set at right angles to the railway with an imposing central block 77ft wide forming the main entrance and carried several feet higher than the wings, the central block to be surmounted by a small tower. The ground floor of both wings was devoted to shops or offices while the upper floor was retained by the company for its staff. The offices included a bombproof control room for supervising all SR territory west of Salisbury. The rooms had light oak doors and wood block flooring. Erecting the building was difficult as it was sited on a steep bank. Conservation of existing amenities was not

Below:
The present-day Central Station (formerly Queen Street) frontage on 23 August 1978. *Author*

Above:
'West Country' Pacific No 21C105
Barnstaple **brings an up express into**
Central station on 27 August 1945.
H. C. Casserley

Left:
No 21C102 *Salisbury* **carrying Exeter**
Central and Exmouth Junction
headcode passes light engine under
the concrete footbridge leading to
New North Road on 31 August 1945.
H. C. Casserley

Below left:
Viewed from the footbridge at the
New North Road end,
'West Country' Pacific No 34038
Lynton **is seen departing with an up**
service on 5 August 1955.
J. Robertson

overlooked as trees bordering the green fronting the new entrance were left in situ. The booking hall, about 45ft square, was approached from the street through one of three pairs of swing doors and inside were a parcels office and cloakroom. There were adjacent bridges crossing the lines, one for passengers and the other for luggage. The former carriage approach road to the down side was adapted to parcels use only. The contract for the building work was let to A. N. Coles Ltd. In September 1931 after the end of summer traffic the offices on the up platform were demolished and November saw the destruction of the wooden offices on the down side. Eighty men were at work and rebuilding the station had the benefit of giving employment to workmen at a time of financial depression.

A special timber built gantry with a working platform measuring 30ft by 40ft was used for demolishing the train shed. The central footbridge obstructed its passage, the question arising of which should be dismantled and re-erected, the gantry, or footbridge. The footbridge lost, and one Sunday half the bridge was cleared away, the gantry moved along the platform on its rollers and the footbridge re-erected. On reaching the east end of the train shed, the gantry was dismantled and taken over to the west end of the down platform and worked its way to the footbridge where the gantry was dismantled this time, re-erected and continued to remove the roof. On the up platform the old refreshment room continued in use despite alterations – it lost its original back wall and ceiling. The rebuilding gave the platforms umbrella roofs.

Top:
Brush Type 4 No D1679 approaches Exeter Central with the 11.30 Paddington-Penzance, diverted via Yeovil due to a derailment at Stoke Canon on 5 July 1969. *R. A. Lumber*

Left:
The banner repeater signal on the up platform at Central. 7 August 1984. *Author*

Above:
The 11.52 Exmouth-Exeter Central, one of the few trains to use the bay platform, most trains continuing down to St David's. 7 August 1984. *Author*

Right:
The 12.35 Exeter Central-Exmouth on 7 August 1984 formed of Class 118 DMU No P467. The doctor is for railway employees. *Author*

Below:
New waiting room on the up platform, Central station. 7 August 1984. *Author*

A 120ft long concrete footbridge which had been made at Exmouth Junction was erected in 12hr on 17 April 1932 at the New North Road entrance to the station. This replaced the old Northernhay entrance and was equipped with a passimeter booking office. Another feature was the train indicator at the entrances at both the Queen Street and New North Road which faced incoming passengers and still displays the platform number for Exmouth trains, these branch trains using various platforms. Another special feature was a machine which in response to pressing a button delivered a card stating times of trains arriving and departing.

The extension of the down platform at the east end making it 950ft in length, benefitted trains on both the main line and in the Exmouth bay. A further improvement was the abolition of the small locomotive depot on the down side at the east end and the utilisation of the space for increasing siding accommodation for the reception and berthing of empty passenger stock and the building of a three road carriage shed. Also provided were additional gas filling pots, standpipes and water hydrants for servicing trains. On 1 July 1933 the Lord Mayor of Exeter formally opened the new main entrance to the new station, renamed Exeter Central, as it could not logically continue to be called Queen Street with an entrance in New North Road. The mayor was presented with a gilt key by the railway. The opening occurred during the week the city celebrated the 800th anniversary of the consecration of the first altar in Exeter Cathedral.

In 1951 a daily average of 800 tickets, excluding seasons, were sold, summer Sundays being the busiest when up to 5,000 passengers used the Exmouth branch. An average of 120 trains stopped or passed through the station each weekday. In 1959 about two million passengers used Exeter Central booking hall. At Central and Exmouth Junction, 1,500 people were employed, earning in 1959 just over £1 million per annum. Buffets on both platforms closed by 5 September 1971. The

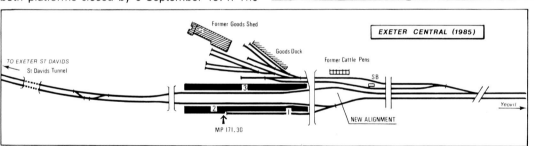

lifting of a facing crossover at the east end of the station in November 1973 confined all down arrivals to the down side and rendered the up bay, Platform No 4, suitable only for departures. Exeter Central became an open station from 19 March 1984, a spin-off of this concept being the re-opening of the New North Road entrance in June that year, closed temporarily during World War 2 and permanently in 1966 to save manpower. Devon County Council defrayed the cost of erecting new signs and lights.

The station was served by horse bus, horse tramcar and later electric tramcar and on 1 June 1903 the first motor bus service ever worked by the LSWR ran between Queen Street and Chagford. Operated by two Milnes-Daimlers, one journey was made each way daily departing from Chagford at 9.15am and Exeter at 2.40pm after the arrival of an express from Waterloo. Short workings were run to Crockernwell. Arrangements were made with Bickford of Exeter to supply horse brakes in the event of a mechanical failure. On 30 September services were withdrawn for the winter, but were resumed in the summer of 1904. The Milnes-Daimlers were replaced by Clarkson steam buses in 1905 and the locomotive superintendent ruled that as they were steam driven, they should be sent to Exmouth Junction for maintenance. In 1908 they were replaced by Thornycroft vehicles and later still by Karriers. After World War 1 pirate

buses siphoned off traffic to such an extent that the railway bus service ran at a loss and so was withdrawn on 20 September 1924. As the Devon General Omnibus & Touring Company based on Exeter competed with the GWR and SR, the two companies shared the business in the proportion Great Western 30% and Southern 20%.

From 24 April to 12 July 1930 the walls of St David's tunnel were refaced, this work necessitating the temporary slewing of tracks towards the centre of the tunnel and imposing single line restriction.

The main line rises from Queen Street to Lion's Holt Halt (0miles 38ch from Queen Street) opened 26 January 1908 with the inauguration of the railmotor service from Exeter to Honiton. On 7 October 1946 it was re-named St James' Park Halt after the nearby Exeter City football ground. The up platform which has a small waiting shelter, is considerably shorter than the down, 119ft compared with 244ft. The station is sited in a cutting and this situation, combined with a rising gradient of 1 in 100, sometimes led to starting problems for up trains.

Below :
Thornycroft bus AA2236 on the LSWR's Queen Street-Chagford service outside Queen Street station c1908.
J. H. Cummings

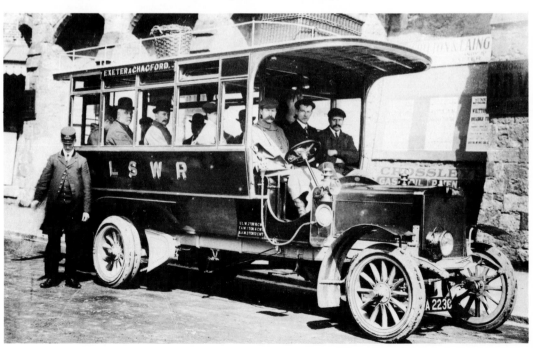

Mount Pleasant Road Halt (0miles 67ch from Queen Street) opened the same day as Lion's Holt Halt, had no waiting shelter. Access was down a steep slope and because of this feature, traffic was light resulting in closure on 2 January 1928. It was sited immediately to the east of the 263yd long brick-lined Black Boy Tunnel. At the inn on Mount Pleasant, Charles II was toasted under his nickname of 'The Black Boy' given on account of his dark complexion, and after the Restoration, the inn sign change to 'Black Boy'.

Above:
The rural appearance of St James' Park halt is apparent in this view on 29 September 1977. Beyond the bridge is Exeter Central up advanced start/Exmouth Junction up distant signal. *Col M. H. Cobb*

Below:
'T9' class 4-4-0 No 716 in original condition passes Mount Pleasant Road halt c1924 with a Waterloo train.
R. A. Lumber collection

Above:
Exmouth Junction reception sidings in 1927 with Mount Pleasant Road halt in the foreground.
Courtesy Railway Engineer

Below:
Unrebuilt 'Battle of Britain' Pacific No 34072 *257 Squadron* leaves Pinhoe with the 12.42pm Exeter Central-Honiton on 2 June 1963. *M. J. Fox*

Whipton Bridge Halt (1mile 50ch from Queen Street) opened on 26 January 1908 and closed 1 January 1923. It was located by the Summer Lane underbridge.

Pinhoe (2miles 46ch from Queen Street) opened on 30 October 1871. Its short platforms were extended in concrete at the down end to hold a six coach train. It closed to passengers 7 March 1966 and to goods 10 January 1967. On 16 May 1983 it was re-opened for an experimental period of three years, the 06.50 Waterloo-Exeter hauled by No 50.007 *Hercules* breaking the ceremonial tape. The cost of re-opening was minimal as the platforms were still in existence so it was just a case of putting in electricity for lighting, repairing the platforms and building a shelter of brick on the down platform. Few people catch an up train from Pinhoe so that a waiting shelter on that platform was not required. Devon County Council provided some of the money to re-open the station.

Double track from Exeter ends east of Pinhoe. Manned half barriers installed on 17 March 1968 replaced the level crossing gates. The first ferro-concrete footbridge on the Southern Railway was erected at Pinhoe to replace a life-expired one of timber. Precast at the company's works at Exmouth Junction, its cost was cheaper than a similar bridge in steel and it did not require painting, with the recurring cost of repainting. The old bridge was demolished in six hours, another 13hr being required for erecting the concrete replacement.

Above:
A crane hoisting the main section of the concrete footbridge into place at Pinhoe. *Courtesy Railway Engineer*

Below:
The re-opened station at Pinhoe, an up view.
Lens of Sutton

Above:
An up view of Polsloe Bridge halt. Exmouth Junction coaling plant can be seen top right. *Lens of Sutton*

Polsloe Bridge Halt (1mile 37ch from Queen Street) on the Exmouth branch was opened on 1 June 1908 with the inauguration of a steam railmotor service from Exeter to Topsham. The original platforms only accommodated a three coach train, but were extended in concrete by the SR just prior to World War 2: the down platform to 488ft and the up to 607ft. Each platform had a waiting shed at the north end whilst another shelter was centrally sited on the down platform only. As the original ticket office served the down platform and was some distance from the path leading to the up, the booking clerk came across with a ticket rack shortly before a train was due. At a later date the ticket office was closed and a ticket booth incorporated in the down platform shelter to which a small porch was added. The halt became unstaffed on 28 February 1965 and the line singled from Exmouth Junction-Topsham between 3-5 February 1973, since which date the up platform

alone has been used, the down line being lifted. In the early 1960s the halt dealt with an average of about 600 passengers daily. During the rush hours, workers would pack the up platform, while on other occasions, the down platform might be crowded with trippers, in fact, until 1964 on Sundays a train for Exmouth actually started from Polsloe Bridge Halt. For the weekend of 27/28 October 1984 Polsloe Bridge became the Exeter terminus for Exmouth line trains during major track work at Central station.

Goods Depots

The original goods shed at St David's built by Hooper of Exeter, was constructed in timber with a slate roof and measured 140ft by 66ft and had four windows in each side. It contained two through and one terminal road. Situated immediately north of the up passenger station, it was replaced by another large timber built shed, still in existence. One of the first economies under Nationalisation was to concentrate all Exeter goods traffic on St David's and in 1951 this depot handled about 200ton of inwards freight daily and outwards roughly 70-80ton. Latterly used by National Carriers, it was more recently used by the S&T Department for storing MAS signalling equipment. The shed was capable of accommodating 20 wagons and contained 15 hand cranes with a capacity of 1½-2ton each to transfer goods between cart and truck. In 1906, 20 goods clerks and 36 porters, checkers, yard foremen were employed, together with a cartage staff of 18 foremen, checkers and carmen. At the north end of the shed the brick built goods offices can still be seen, the clerical work of Alphington Road and also the City Basin depots also being formerly carried out here, while the offices of the goods manager of the Exeter district were situated in Queen Street.

North of the Red Cow level crossing is the former transfer goods shed built of brick. Inside is an island platform, formerly between broad and narrow gauge tracks. It was used from the arrival of mixed gauge in 1876 for the transfer of all traffic from one gauge to the other, all down goods in narrow gauge wagons requiring transhipment. It was no longer needed for transhipment when the broad gauge was finally converted in 1892.

In pursuing the policy of affording special rail connected accommodation and distribution facilities for the use of important traders, in 1930 the GWR provided a depot for Messrs Cadbury on a site adjoining the down main line north of St David's. The building measuring about 75ft by 60ft, had a ground floor stock room at platform level with direct rail access on one side and a covered bay for loading road vehicles at the other. The redbrick building designed by Cadbury's architects, was erected by Messrs Wilkins of Torquay under the supervision of the GWR's divisional engineer. The firm's fresh stock travelled in bulk daily from Bournville to Exeter, the vans being berthed at the depot before noon on the day following despatch. The goods were loaded in containers in covered rail vans to minimise the terminal labour at both ends of the transit. Cadbury's products were delivered onwards to Devon, north and east Cornwall by a fleet of road motor vans specially constructed and decorated to Messrs Cadbury's requirements and supplied by the GWR Road Transport Department. Additionally the GWR's railhead distribution service from Exeter was also used for delivering the products and some of the goods for places further afield were re-despatched

Below:
The east end of the former transfer shed at the down end of Riverside yard on 6 August 1984. *Author*

by rail. As a result of a changeover to combined Cadbury-Fry distribution in 1940 and the subsequent increase in tonnage, the building became inadequate and was replaced by one on the Marsh Barton trading estate. Cadburys now deliver by road.

The original single road goods shed at Queen Street to the north of the passenger station, lasted no longer than 1888 and was replaced by a brick structure measuring 136ft by 30ft and covering two roads. The building was leased to firms soon after Nationalisation, the yard then only dealing with smalls traffic for the city centre. It is still in existence and has attractive metal supports to the canopy roof. The pleasing brick built former weighbridge house still stands at what was the entrance to the goods yard.

Other Depots and Works

The former atmospheric pump house at St David's was later utilised for the manufacture of oil gas used for passenger coach illumination and for cooking in dining cars. St David's was an important gassing station both for the number of trains and from the fact that it was the furthest point west at which oil gas was manufactured. All refreshment cars of down trains which stopped were gassed and watered and optionally, those on up trains. Travelling gas tanks were despatched to all the important stations and branches down to Penzance. Following the closure of the oil gas works at the west end of the Exmouth Junction complex, the SR sent down tank wagons from Central to be filled. The gas was made from oil in a retort heated by a coal fire, dogs and rats being

Below:
'T9' No 30708 arrives at St David's with an up Southern Region passenger train, while Collett '2251' class No 2230 stands in the up bay lines with a gas wagon next to the tender on 30 July 1956. *R. C. Riley*

Bottom:
A '4400' class 2-6-2T heads a City Basin-Riverside Yard transfer freight as it takes the avoiding lines at St David's. The oil gas works is located below the water tank and two gas storage receivers can be seen. *T. Reardon*

unofficially cremated in the furnace. There were seven retorts, up to six being used at a time, the seventh being kept in reserve. They were situated in the former boiler house of the atmospheric pumping station, together with two old locomotive boilers which raised steam to drive the gas compressors, whilst the former engine house became the compressing room containing two horizontal gas compressors of 33hp each, together capable of compressing 3,000 cu ft of gas per hour. The gas passed through condensers and scrubbers to a holder sealed by water. One winter it froze and a chargehand, his wits dulled by cider, threw on a shovel of glowing coals to melt it. The gas was led from the holder and compressed into storage receivers sited at the locomotive shed; opposite Exeter West signal box and one outside the gas house; from which high pressure pipes were laid to gas valves in the station and sidings, the pipes under the railway tracks being specially strengthened. The longest train was gassed completely in five minutes, this time including the fixing and removal of the flexible pipes to every carriage. When the River Exe rose and flooded St David's station, it had the beneficial result of showing up gas leaks undiscovered for years.

Hydrocarbon liquid, a by-product from gas manufacture, was stored in an underground tank and when the hydrocarbon rail tank wagon was being filled, no steam engine was allowed to approach because of the danger of an explosion. Another by-product was oil tar which also was pumped into a rail tank wagon. Every six months, workers at the gas plant were checked by a doctor for cancer warts. Although the workers bathed behind the retort in a bucket of hot water from the boiler before going off duty, they found that the gas penetrated their skin and that when they became warm in bed, gas could be smelled. Fire precautions were stringent: hoses were available and gas workers wore white, fireproof donkey jackets. The retort was continuously manned, even on Christmas Day – two men on the morning shift; two on the late shift and one on night shift. Work at the gas house gradually reduced and it finally closed about 1962 being demolished in 1975. The retort house was lit by town gas, as was the passenger station, oil gas not being suitable.

When the atmospheric engine house was converted to a gasworks, advantage was taken of the height of the building to support a 76,000gall water tank. This involved strengthening the walls. The tank was kept filled by Tangye steam pumps in the adjoining pump house which could deliver up to 25,000gal/hr. Electric pumps were substituted later giving high pressure for fire fighting and low pressure for locomotive use. Water came from a seep well and when the shed received a larger allocation of engines, a pipe was laid directly from the river. When the retort house was demolished, the bricks were pushed down the well. The water tank was cleaned out annually and red oxide applied. In order to keep interference with the

Below:
Class 22 diesel-hydraulic No D6336 passes the water tank at St David's with an up freight on 8 May 1971, in the last year of this class in service. *N. E. Preedy*

operation of the depot to a minimum, this work was carried out on a Sunday from about 6am to 2pm.

Until 1931 a temporary garage in Cowley Road was used for overhauling GWR delivery vans, but was inadequate for the purpose. Messrs C. A. Hayes of Bristol built for £5,000 new premises adjoining the chief goods manager's office opposite St David's station, which were equipped to overhaul 190 delivery vans used in the South-west, eliminating the journey to the main works at Slough, though minor repairs continued to be carried out at Plymouth, Redruth, Taunton and Torre.

The concrete works at Exmouth Junction were started in 1913 by the LSWR chief engineer J. W. Jacomb-Hood, manufacturing concrete post and rail fencing, panel fencing, cable boxes, wicket gates, mile and gradient posts, Meyrick Patent Concrete Railway Sleeper blocks (similar to the concrete pot types which appeared during World War 2) but there was no demand for them due to the time factor required for laying, station nameboards, lamp posts, loading gauge posts, signal wire pulley stakes, saddles for signal rods, trunking for point rodding, crankframes, steps and stringers, platform walls (ie between the edge of the platform surface and the ballast). The area devoted to the manufacture of concrete articles measured 175ft by 1,000ft, advantage being taken of the natural slope of the ground by having all incoming material such as stone chippings, sand and cement for concrete and steel for

reinforcement on the higher level, and the lower siding for the despatch of finished items. The cement was unloaded direct from wagons into the storage shed, Aberthaw being the main supplier, whilst chippings and sand were unloaded by steam crane and grab on to the left and right respectively

Above:
The concrete depot, whose roof covering came from Queen Street station. *Courtesy Railway Engineer*

Below:
Erection of the mechanical coaling plant at Exmouth Junction. *Courtesy Railway Engineer*

of the cement shed. Stone chippings were supplied by Meldon Quarry (though in the WR era they came from Stoneycombe), the sand coming from the estuary of the Taw & Torridge raised by dredger and brought by barge to Fremington where it was unloaded into wagons. The hopper of the electric cement mixer was level with the floor of the shed and so the constituents for the mix could easily be barrowed to the hopper. Mixed concrete was distributed to different areas of the yard by means of hand pushed trolleys running on 2ft gauge flat bottomed track. William Holt Shortt, the divisional engineer, was a brilliant man and from 1928 onwards the works began to expand. Shortt designed concrete footbridges, whilst additional items manufactured from concrete were sectional buildings, cable posts, telegraph posts, signal posts, yard lighting poles, with air raid shelters being added to the list in World War 2. The works were particularly busy when an electrification scheme was in progress, Exmouth Junction providing all concrete items. Before 1939 there

Above:
A scene at the concrete works c1937.
C. W. Wood collection

were 140 employees, while the number increased in the postwar period to a maximum of 186. In BR times Exmouth Junction products went further afield, one concrete bridge going to Maesteg and another to Hull.

Concrete tubes were scientifically tested in the laboratory for strength. Latterly the works were divided into various sections: carpenters, fibreglass, and reinforcement. It closed in 1963 under rationalisation as Taunton had been set up as a pre-stressed concrete depot and therefore one depot was superfluous. Residents used to grumble about the cement dust from the concrete works, and then when it closed, they complained of dust from the coal concentration depot set up on its site. Steel principals and stanchions for the concrete sheds at Exmouth Junction came from Queen Street station when it was demolished.

Top:
The exterior of the Carriage & Wagon Shops on 7 August 1984. *Author*

Above:
A view inside the Carriage & Wagon shops at Exmouth Junction on 7 August 1984. *Author*

New carriage and wagon shops opened at Exmouth Junction in 1928 were planned in two bays: 350ft by 51½ft and 300ft by 51½ft, ferro concrete construction being employed. Six roads ran into the shops, three in each bay, one road being provided with a pit for examining the undersides of vehicles. The shop dealt with running repairs to carriages and wagons on the Western Division. Rivetting made a deafening noise. The works employed over 120 men in 1948, over 60 men until July 1983 when the number shrank to about 10. Most of the machinery was removed later that year, the wheel lathe being taken from the wagon shop in August 1984. Today the Area civil engineer based at Exeter Central in the former Southern Railway offices covers the area from west of Bruton, Durston and Sherborne to Penzance.

Signalling

At Exeter the GWR had eight busy signalboxes within a little over two miles. Cowley Bridge Junction was a class B box situated where the GWR main line and the LSWR line to Barnstaple and Plymouth divided, had a 44 lever frame and until the 1960s a regulator was employed to control traffic through St David's. The box was lengthened in 1943 when Riverside Yard was extended towards Cowley Bridge. The extension was identifiable by the fact that the nameplate remained in the centre of what was the original box length. The former LSWR line over the two river bridges was singled on 28 November 1965, but

remained double beyond there until singled on 15/16 December 1984 when a new panel was commissioned at Crediton. Exeter East, a class 1 signal box with 52 levers, at one time controlled the exit from the yard. Destroyed during World War 2 it was replaced by a new box on 17 June 1942, while Exeter Riverside, a class 2 box, opened 2 July 1943, the box itself came from Hatherley Junction, Cheltenham, had 53 levers and controlled a new

Above left:
Electric capstan for shunting operations. Exmouth Junction Carriage & Wagon shops on 7 August 1984. *Author*

Left:
Rails used to protect a cast iron drain pipe at Exmouth Junction. 7 August 1984. *Author*

yard opened on 25 October 1943. The East box and Riverside faced each other across six roads, many of their points and signals being electrically interlocked. East box closed on 22 November 1973 and Riverside on 5 April 1981. Exeter Middle, a class C box, with 95 levers, controlled the east end of St David's station as well as the lengthy Red Cow level crossing which at one time crossed no less

Top:
Three-car DMU No P469 towing a former GWR Siphon van on a Barnstaple-Exeter service crosses the Exe on the approach to Cowley Bridge junction on 1 June 1977.
Col M.H. Cobb

Above:
A 'Peak' brings the down 'Cornishman' past Exeter East up starter and Cowley Bridge up distant, with the distant off for the 12.55 departure to Barnstaple on 8 November 1973.
Col M. H. Cobb

than 14 tracks including goods lines, now reduced to five. Opened on 5 July 1915 it replaced a 90 lever box standing between the up and down main lines. Owing to limited ground space, Exeter Middle box stood on a comparatively narrow brickwork base and oversailed at floor level. There was radio communication between the Exeter ex-GWR signal boxes, Riverside yard and St David's station, but not Central. The box was manned by a signalman on three shifts and a telegraphist on the two daytime shifts. In the 1950s an additional signalman worked on summer Saturdays. The city council pay for a crossing attendant to direct foot passengers through when the lifting barriers are lowered. For safety, the signalman was required to advise the crossing attendant when a movement in a wrong direction was to take place.

Above:
Exeter Middle box on 16 August 1975 showing the unusual construction, with tracks passing close on both sides. The line on this rear side was later removed. *Col M. H. Cobb*

Right:
Cabin for crossing attendant at Red Cow level crossing on 6 August 1984. *Author*

Below:
'G6' class 0-6-0Ts Nos E237 and E257 with 'T9' class No E724 descend into St David's past Exeter West box on 25 May 1929. *H. C. Casserley*

Above:
A Class 50 passes Exeter Middle box with an up train on 6 August 1984. *Author*

Left:
Class 47 No 47.027 with an up express emits a plume of smoke as it passes Exeter Middle box down home gantry on 16 August 1975. *Col M. H. Cobb*

Bottom:
Class 35 'Hymek' No D7066 leaves platform 3 at St David's on the 13.50 Ilfracombe-Paddington on 6 September 1969. *R. A. Lumber*

Under MAS, there is closed-circuit television (CCTV) for the crossing, the attendant still continuing to be employed. At the west end of the level crossing and nine roads from Middle box was Exeter Goods Yard box, a class 4 box, containing five levers, its main task being to protect the crossing. In 1945 it was open continuously except 10pm Sundays until 6am Mondays. It closed 25 February 1978 when the goods avoiding line tracks were severed.

Exeter West class D, was the largest box in the area with 113 levers. In addition to controlling the west end of St David's, it worked the entrance to the engine shed, the incline to Exeter Central and at one time the entrance and exit of the goods lines

Above right:
Not often photographed but full of character was Exeter Goods yard signalbox, situated beside the continuation of Red Cow level crossing over the freight avoiding lines. Seen on 8 November 1973. *Col M. H. Cobb*

Right:
A DMU leaving platform 4 for Central station. Note the platform 4 starting signal indicating 'UP CEN'. 16 August 1975. *Col. M. H. Cobb*

Below:
A rear view of Exeter West box, next to which is LSWR milepost 172, on 16 August 1975. *Col M. H. Cobb*

Left:
**No 47.002 at the head of the
St Austell-Crewe Motorail service
passing Exeter West up home gantry
on 16 August 1975. This gantry was
replaced on 23 November 1975.**
Col M. H. Cobb

Left:
**The new gantry is passed by Class 46
No 46.005 approaching St David's
with an up 'all stations' from
Paignton on 4 June 1976. The road is
set for platform 6. This gantry was in
turn to disappear under the
resignalling of 1985.** *Col M. H. Cobb*

Left:
**A class 33 locomotive with an up
Exeter-Waterloo service climbs the
1 in 37 past Exeter West advanced
starter on 16 August 1975.**
Col M. H. Cobb

avoiding the passenger station. A new frame with 131 levers was installed in 1958. In 1984 it was worked by a signalman for thres shifts and a telegraphist on the two daytime shifts. On summer Saturdays in the 1950s it was manned by two signalmen and a booking boy. The box has been preserved by the Exeter West Group. Exeter St Thomas, a class 4 box, with its 15 lever frame, stood on the down platform inside the train shed. In 1945 it opened 6am-10pm and was closed all day Sundays. It closed permanently on 19 April 1959, but had previously been shut as a wartime economy measure from November 1917 until October 1921. The original City Basin Junction signalbox, class 3 with its 33 lever frame, as well as controlling the main line, was responsible for the junction of the Teign Valley branch and also the Exeter Basin Junction. Closed 9 December 1962 it was replaced by Exeter City Basin signalbox with 27 levers, class B, situated to the north, only open 08.00-16.00 shift, the signalman's wages partly paid for by King's Asphalt.

In addition to the standard bell code, local codes were used for movements peculiar to the area in order to avoid time-wasting telephone calls.

SPECIAL BELL CODES, EXETER WEST TO EXETER MIDDLE, 1938

IS LINE CLEAR FOR?

G W express passenger train not booked to stop at
Exeter   3-3-3
(To terminate at West box for down trains)
G W express train not booked to stop at Newton
Abbot, (via Dainton for Plymouth)   3-3-3
(via Kingskerwell) – To be started by West
box   3-3-1
Southern Railway Passenger or mixed train   5-1
Southern Railway breakdown van train or light
engine going to assist a disabled train   7-3
Southern Railway freight or ballast train   3-4-1
Southern Railway light engine other than an
assisting engine   1-5
Southern Railway empty coaching stock train   7-2
Southern Railway assisting (banker) engine   1-2-4
G W light engine to or from Loco Yard between
East and West boxes   2-3-4
G W light engine between West and Middle or
Middle and East, or vice versa   2-3-2
Engine with vehicles attached (pilot)   2-2-4
City Basin freight   4-3
May an engine with or without vehicles run down
the up line?   4-2

May an engine with or without vehicles run up the
down line?   1-6
May an engine with or without vehicles set back
through the scissors Down platform to Through
line (to be rung out on platform line bell)   1-4-1
May an engine with or without vehicles set back
through scissors. Through line to platform line?
(To be rung out on T.L. bell).   1-4-1

SPECIAL CODES AT EXETER WEST

May a passenger train enter section already
occupied?   2-4-2
May a train shunt towards your home signal?   3-3-1
Shunting into forward section completed   5-2
Exe and Teign Valley trains   4-2-2

NOTE – Southern Railway trains from Cowley Bridge Junction to Exeter are *up* trains and Southern Railway trains from Exeter to Cowley Bridge are *down* trains, but the down G W R regulations apply to Up S R trains and vice-versa.

SPECIAL CODES AT COWLEY BRIDGE JUNCTION

IS LINE CLEAR FOR?

Southern Railway power-worked trolley or
inspection car
Running through section   1-4-2
Requiring to stop in section   2-4-1
To be used only between Cowley Bridge Jcn and Newton St Cyres, or Crediton if Newton St Cyres is switched out

Cullompton signal box 12½ miles distant on the up line advised Exeter West box of all down trains not calling at St David's by a 1-2-1 code and in similar fashion, Exeter Middle box reported to Newton Abbot box all trains not stopping at Newton, ringing 3-3-3 for Plymouth trains and 3-3-1 for those for the Kingswear branch.

The LSWR had three signal boxes at Queen Street: 'A' box at the east end of the passenger and goods station complex; 'B' at the east end of the passenger station and 'C' at the west end of the passenger station and at the head of the gradient from St David's. The original box nearer the tunnel, was replaced by one between the platforms by 1888. With the rebuilding of Queen Street into Exeter Central, Exeter Central 'A' box, situated at the east end of the layout had a 90 lever frame (in later years severely rationalised), opened 15 June 1927 and operated with one signalman and a booking boy, while 'B' box, opened on 13 September 1925 with a 35 lever frame, was at the head of the gradient up from St David's. Operated by one man, it closed on 23 February 1970. Only a locomotive and nine bogie coaches could be held at the down starter and clear Platform 2, and on summer Saturdays when trains were liable to be held there, engines were loaded to 12 or 13 bogies. 'B' box could not accept 'line clear' from St David's until the acceptance of 'line clear' from 'A' box, because of the difficulty a train would have experienced starting on a gradient of 1 in 37, not to speak of the danger of slipping back and being derailed on one of the three sets of catch points.

On 13 October 1984 the down through road was taken out of use and a small panel unit temporarily installed in the box a week later. The eastern extension to the up platform was removed and what is left of the former No 4 platform road now

forms a run round loop for freight locomotives before propelling wagons into the yard sidings. Just four colour light signals – 3 up and 4 down – comprise the station's complement. The down road at the approach to Black Boy Tunnel has a 4-aspect signal.

As there is no traffic from midnight until about 5am, laterly Exeter Central box was manned only for two shifts like the two other ex-Southern Railway boxes in the Exeter area. To facilitate movements at the station, all four through roads were signalled for running in either direction.

Exmouth Junction, a B class box, as well as controlling the branch and main lines, controlled the marshalling yard, motive power depot, carriage and wagon shops and concrete works. The old twice-enlarged signal box, latterly with a 49 lever Stevens frame, was replaced by a modern box with a 64 lever Westinghouse A3 frame on 17 November

Left:
The former Exeter Central B signalbox sited next to the Queen Street road bridge at the top of the famous incline from St David's. The box closed on 23 February 1974.
Author

Below:
Two Class 42 'Warship' diesel-hydraulics, Nos D804 *Avenger* and D808 *Centaur* on a return SLS special from the Dart Valley Railway pass Exeter Central A signalbox on 17 May 1969. *R. A. Lumber*

1959. It has catch handle locking actuation and 'L' type lever locks and circuit controllers. Branch signalling was by three-position block using standard BR (SR) instruments, and was superseded from 5 February 1973 by the Tokenless Block System worked by acceptance lever with continuous track circuiting. The siting and original equipment of the box made provision for future access to the proposed DEMU depot, which in the event, was never built. The basic structure of the new cabin was load-carrying brickwork with reinforced concrete floors on steel frame supports. When the Exeter MAS box takes over control of the Exmouth branch in 1987, the box will remain, but have a panel and not levers. Pinhoe box, class A, a typical LSWR cabin, controls the level crossing and is at the point where the double line from Exeter became single on 11 June 1967. It has 17 levers in the frame, of which 9 are working. The single line is worked on the Tokenless Block System and ultimately singling will extend through Pinhoe station.

Mechanical signalling in the Exeter area was replaced by the MAS power box which came into use over the Bank Holiday weekend on 5 May 1985, covering Exeter City Basin to Stoke Canon and Exmouth Junction, and began with Cowley Bridge-Crediton on 16 December 1984. The contract for £833,515 was awarded to Woodman Ltd, of Exeter, work starting early in 1983. Isis

Construction completing the building. Territory covered by the box will be gradually extended and will be fully commissioned in 1988, finally controlling 212 main line and 77 subsidiary signals, 149 points and replacing some 30 mechanical lever boxes between Somerton and Totnes, some more than 90 years old. All platforms at St David's are signalled for two way working. Platforms Nos 1 & 3 are now for arrival and departure of Exeter Central, Exmouth and Salisbury trains, No 4 being the down main, up trains to Paddington using Nos 5 & 6. Visual display units on the platforms and controlled from the panel box, give train service and platform information.

Carriage Stabling Facilities

Carriage sheds were a feature of Exeter until relatively recent times, the SDR carriage shed near the down end of platform 1 at St David's being demolished in 1980. It was used for stabling rolling stock used for local working west of Exeter, while stock in the sidings between the station and the river, was for local trips to the east. The B&E carriage shed was between the down platform and Red Cow level crossing, being pulled down in 1909 when the platform was lengthened. The Southern Railway built a three road carriage shed in 1930 at the up end of the down platform at Queen Street. Coaches for up trains were stabled in the west sidings, also the Exeter cars from the 'Devon Belle'; stock for down trains and the Exmouth branch being kept in the shed or the two adjacent sidings. A total of 73 coaches could be berthed in Central's various carriage sidings.

Above:
Adams '0415' class 4-4-2T No 30583 arrives at Exeter Central with an Ian Allan railtour on 12 April 1953. The carriage sheds on the right feature a collection of elderly pre-grouping stock. On the left a Bulleid Pacific blows off at the long up platform. *J. H. Bamsey*

Left:
The derelict South Devon carriage shed at St David's seen on 3 May 1977, a month before its demolition. The site of the shed and former South Devon sidings is now largely occupied by new buildings attached to the post office sorting depot.
Col M. H. Cobb

Below left:
Ivatt 2-6-2T No 41249, one of a number which operated in the West Country, engaged in carriage shunting duties at Exeter Central on 18 May 1965 during the final week of passenger steam working. This view from the Queen Street road bridge clearly shows the lines to St David's dropping sharply away to the right.
R. A. Lumber

Above:
'E1/R' class 0-6-2T No 32124 pilots 'N' class 2-6-0 No 31845 up the bank into Exeter Central on 26 September 1958 with another 'E1/R' banking. *P. Q. Treloar*

Left:
Two 'E1/R' tank locomotives Nos 32124 & 32135 prepare to assist a train of ballast from Meldon Quarry up the incline to Central from the centre road at St David's on 4 October 1957. *P. Q. Treloar*

The Incline

When a banking locomotive was required to assist a train from St David's to Central, the person in charge of the Middle platform rang a tremulous bell and actuated a visual indicator to the signalman in the Middle box that a banker was required, he then set the points for the engine to run from the bankers' siding in front of his box, to the rear of the train. On a summer Saturday, almost every SR express was of a weight which demanded rear end assistance and returning bankers had to cut across the down main line to their lay-by. To save paths, SR down trains came from Central triple- or quadruple-headed, returning bankers ahead of the train engine, four locomotives being the limit. Bankers in the 1950s were Class 'E1/R' 0-6-2Ts, together sometimes with 'M7' 0-4-4Ts; Class 'Z' 0-8-0Ts appeared in 1959, Class 'W' 2-6-4Ts in 1962 and in 1963 when the WR had taken control, 0-6-0PTs. The headcode a banker carried from St David's to Central was one disc in the centre of the buffer beam.

Special instructions were issued for working the gradient of 1 in 37 for both the up and down directions. On summer Saturdays particularly, there was much question and answer crowing of bankers and train engines. Today diesel hauled passenger trains are virtually never banked, whilst freight trains requiring assistance are provided with a banker of whatever type is available.

On arrival of up trains at Eggesford and Okehampton, the guard was required to advise the stationmaster for transmission to Exeter Central, of the class of engine and tonnage of the train from St David's to Central. A train was not allowed to be divided on the incline and in the event of it coming to a stand, brakes were required to be fully applied pending the arrival of an assistant engine. The Central stationmaster was required to appoint a competent person to walk over the incline once each week and see that a sufficient number of sprags for applying wagon brakes were provided at suitable intervals.

Extract From British Railways (Southern Region) Appendix to Working Timetables, 1960

WORKING OF TRAINS FROM EXETER CENTRAL TO EXETER ST. DAVID'S. – Not more than four engines, including the train engine, must be attached to any passenger or freight train.

Freight.– Trains must not exceed a load equal to 45 loaded wagons, exclusive of brake vans or, in number, 43 vehicles.

Except where otherwise provided in these instructions, all trains leaving Exeter Central must have brake vans attached of not less tonnage that shown below for the respective loads, and a man must ride in each van:–

Load of train, exclusive of brake vans	Minimum tonnage of brake van or vans
Not exceeding equal to 25 loaded wagons	20 tons
Above 25 and not exceeding equal to 30 loaded wagons	25 tons
Above 30 and not exceeding equal to 45 loaded wagons	40 tons

Before leaving Exeter Central the guard must advise the driver the formation and the load of the train and agree with him as to the number of hand brakes to be applied, to enable the train to be brought to a stand on any part of the incline. The hand brakes must be applied on the near side on vehicles nearest the engine and the driver must satisfy himself that this has been done. The guard must see that the brakes are released at Exeter St David's.

Four or more fitted 4-wheeled vehicles attached next the engine with the continuous brake connected and in working order, can be considered equivalent to a brake van and the brake power of the train can be calculated accordingly. The guard must advise the driver the number of fitted vehicles so connected.

When it is necessary for an additional brake van to be attached to a train which has no fitted vehicles connected to the engine, the attachment must be next to the engine and a second guard provided.

The second guard must release the van brakes and any hand brakes applied on wagons, and advise the driver and guard.

NOTE:- The foregoing instructions do not apply to a fitted empty stone train to Meldon Quarry with a maximum load of 20 large 40 ton hopper wagons and 4 brake vans provided the brake is connected and in working order throughout the train.

The yard foreman will be responsible for seeing that trains are properly equipped with brake power before being despatched from Exmouth Junction and in the case of trains not calling at Exmouth junction the inspector or foreman at Exeter Central will be responsible in this respect.

ASSISTANCE OF UP TRAINS. – The undermentioned instructions in regard to the assistance of trains from Exeter St David's to Exeter Central are supplementary to those appearing in Table "J".

Up Fully Fitted Trains (excluding fully fitted freight and ballast trains). – The arrangements governing the provision of additional engine power on up passenger and fully fitted parcel, van and similar type non-passenger carrying trains from Exeter St Davids to Exeter Central are shown below:-

The loads of up passenger and fully fitted parcel, van and similar type non-passenger carrying trains should not exceed 400-tons, equivalent to 12 bogie coaches, except by special authority.

The hauling capacity of the various types of locomotives working over this section of line is:-

Class of Locomotive	Power Classification	Maximum single engine load between Exeter St David's and Exeter Central
W R /D 63xx	—	130 tons
W R 57xx	—	140 tons*
L M 2 (2-6-2T)	2P	140 tons*
M 7	2P	140 tons
T 9	3P	140 tons
BR Std 3 (2-6-2T)	3P	165 tons
BR Std 3	3P	165 tons
BR Std 4	4P	165 tons
U	4P	165 tons
N	4P	200 tons
Z	6F	200 tons
W C	7P	200 tons
B O B	7P	200 tons
W R 43xx	4 MT	200 tons
53xx	4 MT	200 tons
63xx	4 MT	200 tons
73xx	4 MT	200 tons

* When used for banking purposes the combined load can be increased by 30 tons.

An assisting engine or engines to be provided when the weight of the train exceeds the hauling capacity of the train engine.

Assisting engines (at front or rear if the load is not more than 200 tons and at rear if over 200 tons) to be provided, the type of assisting engine to be determined by adding together the hauling capacity of the train engine and the assisting engine.

In computing the weight of the trains, the tare weight of passenger stock or fitted goods vehicles to be used; loaded or empty containers the combined tare of the wagon and container; empty milk tanks the tare weight; loaded milk tanks the tare weight plus 15 tons.

The assisting engine or engines at the rear of a train must be coupled to the train and the continuous brake pipes must also be coupled throughout. Such engine or engines must only push slightly until the train has passed through the crossings at the foot of the incline.

In cases where an assisting engine is not provided at the rear of a train, the rear vehicle must be a vehicle with a brake compartment, in which a guard must ride, except in cases where the rear vehicle or vehicles do not convey passengers and there is a vehicle with a brake compartment with a man in charge next in front; in such cases the rear vehicle or vehicles must be fitted with the vacuum brake complete.

When the load or formation of any up passenger train necessitates additional engine power on the incline, or should the driver of a train make request for such additional power, telephonic advices must be sent, as under, to ensure that the requisite engine or engines are in readiness upon arrival of the train at Exeter St Davids.

Telephonic advice must be given immediately after departure of the train to the signalman at Exeter Central B signal box stating train, type of engine or engines (4P, 7P, etc,) tonnage, also if the rear vehicle conveying passengers has no brake van behind it or contains no brake compartment with man in charge, or vehicles not fully vacuum fitted attached behind the rear brake vehicle in which a guard is riding.

The Electrification Scheme

At the meeting of the Great Western Board on 1 May 1925, Sir Felix Pole proposed that a consulting engineer, Sir Philip Dawson, prepare a scheme for electrification of a GWR main line. His report suggested the electrification of all lines west of Taunton. No further action was taken but on 11 February 1938 Sir James Milne at a board meeting proposed that in view of the increasing cost of steam working, Messrs Merz & McLellan, consulting engineers, should be engaged to investigate the economic advantages of electrifying the company's system west of Taunton. The subsequent report led the directors to drop the idea. The severe gradients and curves would have limited speeds possible with electrification; the bulk of the mileage was run in summer and tended to be concentrated into a few hours on Saturdays, this factor involving a higher expenditure on fixed equipment and locomotives than if traffic flow had been uniform; because of the unusually high proportion of curved to straight track, shorter than normal distances would have been required between gantries carrying the overhead wires; traffic density on branches was insufficient to warrant their electrification, preventing the area from going entirely over to a new form of traction. It was estimated that about 164 electric locomotives would have been required, replacing an equal number of steam engines. The net cost of electrifying the lines was over £4 million, whilst the balance of saving in working costs available for interest on net capital expenditure was calculated to be 0.75%.

One gains the impression that the GWR directors wished to appear progressive, but right from the start had no serious intention of electrification, setting themselves limits which were bound to produce a negative conclusion eg no allowance was made for any increase in fixed receipts.

Locomotive Allocations

Exeter GWR Allocation 1914

0-4-2T '517' class
559
1433
1439
1440
1466

0-6-0T '1076' class
737
1245
1620
1654

0-6-0 'Standard Goods'
782
1197

2-4-0ST ex South Devon Railway
1300 (formerly *Mercury*)

0-6-0T '1854' class
1751

0-6-0T '850' class
1932
1956

0-6-0 Dean Goods
2305
2445
2456
2544
2560
2563

2-6-0 'Aberdare' class
2621

4-6-0 'Saint' class
2917 *Saint Bernard*
2925 *Saint Martin*
2933 *Bibury Court*
2939 *Croome Court*
2975 *Viscount Churchill*
2988 *Rob Roy*

2-6-2T '3100' class
3118
3132

4-4-0 'Duke' class
3272 *Fowey*
3285 *Katerfelto*

4-4-0 'City' class
3709 *Quebec*

4-4-0 'County' class
3806 *County Kildare*
3827 *County of Gloucester*

4-6-0 'Star' class
4037 *Queen Philippa*

4-4-0 'Atbara' class
4122 *Colonel Edgcumbe*

Total 37

No railmotors

Exeter GWR Allocation 8 January 1938

0-6-0PT '1854' class
1897

0-6-0PT '850' class
1930
1956

0-6-0PT '2021' class
2148

4-4-0 'Bulldog' class
3395 *Tasmania*
3451 *Pelican*

4-6-0 'Castle' class
4076 *Carmarthen Castle*
4098 *Kidwelly Castle*
4099 *Kilgerran Castle*
5003 *Lulworth Castle*
5026 *Criccieth Castle*
5059 *Earl St Aldwyn*
5065 *Newport Castle*

2-6-2T '4400' class
4405

2-6-2T '4500' class
4530
5543
5541

2-8-0 '4700' class
4707

0-4-2T Collett
4805
4819
4827
4832
4835
4840
4849
4851
4868
4869

4-6-0 'Grange' class
6813 *Eastbury Grange*
6814 *Enborne Grange*
6822 *Manton Grange*
6825 *Llanvair Grange*

0-6-0PT '5700' class
7716
7761

2-6-0 '4300' class
8338
8361

0-6-0PT '8750' class
9718

Total 37

Exeter GWR Allocation 31 December 1947

4-6-0 'County' class
1020 *County of Monmouth*

0-4-2T Collett
1405
1429
1435
1440
1449
1451
1468
1469

0-6-0PT '2021' class
2088

0-6-0 '2251' class
2230

2-8-0 '2800' class
2873
3834

4-4-0 'Bulldog' class
3335
3395 *Tasmania*
3451 *Pelican*

0-6-0PT '8750' class
3603
3606
3794
9646
9647

4-6-0 'Star' class
4054 *Princess Charlotte*

4-6-0 'Castle' class
5012 *Berry Pomeroy Castle*
5059 *Earl St Aldwyn*
5098 *Clifford Castle*

2-6-2T '4400' class
4410

2-6-2T '4500' class
4530
5525

2-8-0 '4700' class
4706

2-6-0 '4300' class
5321
6301
6397
7316

0-6-0PT '5700' class
5760
7716
7761

4-6-0 'Hall' class
5902 *Howick Hall*

Total 37

Exeter Western Region Allocation March 1959

0-4-2T Collett
1440
1451
1462
1468
1471

0-6-0PT '5700' class
3606
3794
7716
9629
9765

2-6-2T '5100' class
4117

2-6-2T '4500' class
4589
5546

4-6-0 'Hall' class
4944 *Middleton Hall*
4948 *Northwick Hall*
4960 *Pyle Hall*
4992 *Crosby Hall*
5959 *Mawley Hall*
6965 *Thirlestaine Hall*

2-6-0 '4300' class
5339
6385
7311
7316

0-6-0PT '5400' class
6412

0-6-0PT '9400' class
9439
9474
9497

Total 27

Southern Railway Exmouth Junction Allocation 1933

0-4-2 'A12' class
611
640
643
644

0-4-2T 'D1' class
2359
3633

0-6-2T 'E1/R' class
2096
2135
2695

0-6-0T 'G6' class
237
259
267
278

4-4-0 'K10' class
135
392

4-4-0 'L11' class
154
159

0-4-4T 'M7' class
35
37
41
42
44
45
133
247
253
320
328
356
374
375
669
671

2-6-0 'N' class
1406
1826
1827
1828
1830
1831
1832
1835
1836
1837
1838
1839
1840
1841
1842
1843
1844
1845
1846
1847
1848
1849

1852
1853
1854
1855
1857
1858
1859
1860

4-6-0 'N15 King Arthur' class
448 *Sir Tristram*
449 *Sir Torre*
740 *Merlin*
743 *Lyonesse*
744 *Maid of Astolat*
746 *Pendragon*
747 *Elaine*
768 *Sir Balin*
769 *Sir Balan*

0-4-4T '02' class
187
195
196
198
199
214
228
232
236

4-4-0 'S11' class
396
399
401
403

4-6-0 'S15' class
823
824
825
826
827

4-4-0 'T9' class
117
283
703
710
711
717
719
723
732

0-6-0 '700' class
326
689
693

0-6-0 '0395' class
3029
3083
3433
3436

4-4-2T '0415' class
3125
3520

0-8-0T 'Z' class
954

Total 109

Southern Railway Exmouth Junction Allocation January 1947

0-4-4T 'M7' class
24
30
34
37
39
46
49
55
105
124
133
245
252
253
255
256
320
323
356
374
375
376
377
668
669
671

0-4-4T '02' class
192
193
199
207
224
230
232

0-6-2T 'E1/R class
2124
2135
2695
2697

4-4-2T '0415' class
3125
3488
3520

0-8-0T 'Z' class
954

0-6-0 '0395' class
3029

4-4-0 'K10' class
135
137
138
329

4-4-0 'L11' class
156
408
409
411
436
439

4-4-0 'T9' class
282
283
301
722
723
724
725
730

2-6-0 'N' class
1407
1408
1409
1828
1831
1832
1833
1834
1835
1836
1837
1838
1839
1840
1841
1842
1845
1847
1853
1855
1856
1869
1871
1875

4-6-0 'S15' class
823
824
825
826
827
844
845
846
847

4-6-2 'Merchant Navy' class
21C1 *Channel Packet*
21C2 *Union Castle*
21C3 *Royal Mail*
21C4 *Cunard White Star*
21C5 *Canadian Pacific*

4-6-2 'West Country' class
21C101 *Exeter*
21C102 *Salisbury*
21C103 *Plymouth*
21C104 *Yeovil*
21C105 *Barnstaple*
21C106 *Bude*
21C107 *Wadebridge*
21C108 *Padstow*

21C109 *Lyme Regis*
21C110 *Sidmouth*
21C111 *Tavistock*
21C112 *Launceston*
21C113 *Okehampton*
21C114 *Budleigh Salterton*
21C115 *Exmouth*
21C116 *Bodmin*
21C117 *Ilfracombe*
21C118 *Axminster*
21C119 *Bideford*
21C120 *Seaton*
21C141 *Wilton*
21C142 *Dorchester*
21C143 *Combe Martin*
21C144 *Woolacombe*
21C145 *Ottery St Mary*
21C146 *Braunton*
21C147 *Callington*

Total 125

Southern Region Exmouth Junction Allocation May 1959

0-4-4T 'M7' class
30021
30023
30024
30025
30027
30044
30045
30323
30374
30667
30668
30669
30670
30676

0-4-4T '02' class
30182
30199
30232

0-6-0 '700' class
30317
30327
30691

4-4-2T '0415' class
30582
30583
30584

4-4-0 'T9' class
30702
30709
30711
30715
30717
30726

4-6-0 'S15' class
30841
30842
30843
30844
30845
30846

0-8-0T 'Z' class
30950
30953
30955
30956
30957

2-6-0 'U' class
31790
31791

2-6-0 'N' class
31830
31831
31832
31833
31834
31835
31836
31837
31838
31839
31840
31841
31842
31843
31844
31845
31846
31847
31849

0-6-2T 'E1/R' class
32697

4-6-2 'West Country' class
34002 *Salisbury*
34011 *Tavistock*
34015 *Exmouth*
34023 *Blackmore Vale*
34024 *Tamar Valley*
34030 *Watersmeet*
34032 *Camelford*
34033 *Chard*
34034 *Honiton*
34035 *Shaftesbury*
34036 *Westward Ho*
34038 *Lynton*
34096 *Trevone*
34104 *Bere Alston*
34106 *Lydford*
34108 *Wincanton*

4-6-2 'Battle of Britain' class
34056 *Croydon*
34057 *Biggin Hill*
34058 *Sir Frederick Pile*
34060 *25 Squadron*
34061 *73 Squadron*
34062 *17 Squadron*
34063 *229 Squadron*
34069 *Hawkinge*
34072 *257 Squadron*
34074 *46 Squadron*
34075 *264 Squadron*
34076 *41 Squadron*
34079 *141 Squadron*
34080 *74 Squadron*
34081 *92 Squadron*
34109 *Sir Trafford Leigh-Mallory*
34110 *66 Squadron*

4-6-2 'Merchant Navy' class
35003 *Royal Mail*
35008 *Orient Line*
35009 *Shaw Savill*
35011 *General Steam Navigation*
35013 *Blue Funnel*
35023 *Holland-Afrika Line*
35026 *Lamport & Holt Line*

2-6-2T Class 2MT
41306
41307
41318

2-6-2T Class 3MT
82010
82011
82013
82017
82018
82019
82022
82023
82024
82025

Total 115

Southern Region Exmouth Junction Allocation May 1965

0-6-0PT '5700' class
4655
4666
4694
9647

2-6-2T Class 2MT
41206
41216
41223
41249
41291
41307
41317
41321

4-6-0 Class 4MT
75008
75022
75025

2-6-4T Class 4MT
80037
80041
80064

2-6-2T Class 3MT
82030
82039
82040
82042
82044

Total 23

Bibliography

Ahrons, E. L; *Locomotive & Train Working in the latter part of the Nineteenth Century:* Vols 4 & 5; Heffer, 1952

Allen, C. J; *Titled Trains of the Western;* Ian Allan Ltd, 1974

Allen, G. F; *Resorts for Railfans: Exeter Central & Exmouth Junction;* Trains Illustrated pp379-85, 1952

Allen, G. F; *Resorts for Railfans: Exeter St David's;* Trains Illustrated pp382-7, 1953

Allen, G. F; *The Western Since 1948;* Ian Allan Ltd, 1974

Arthurton, A. W; *Notable Railway Stations: St David's, Exeter;* Railway Magazine, October 1907

Arthurton, A. W; *The Principal Stations of the Great Western Railway. No 1 Exeter;* Great Western Railway Magazine pp63-6 1906

Beavor, E. S; *Steam Motive Power Depots;* Ian Allan Ltd, 1983

Bolger, P; *BR Steam Motive Power Depots WR;* Ian Allan Ltd, 1983

Bolger, P; *BR Steam Motive Power Depots SR;* Ian Allan Ltd, 1983

Bradley, D. L; *Locomotives of the London & South Western Railway:* Vols 1 & 2 RCTS 1965/67

Bradshaw's Railway Guides, (various dates).

Clinker, C. R; *Closed Stations & Goods Depots,* Avon-Anglia, 1978

Cobb, M. H; *Is it a distant?* Railway Magazine, October 1978

Cooke, R. A; *Track Layout Diagrams of the GWR and BR WR,* Sections 14 & 15; Author, 1974

Cummings, J; *Railway Motor Buses and Bus Services in the British Isles 1902-1933,* Vol 2; Oxford Publishing Company, 1980

Gregory, R. H; *The South Devon Railway;* Oakwood Press, 1982

Hadfield, C; *The Canals of South West England;* David & Charles, 1967

Hateley, R; *Industrial Locomotives of South Western England;* Industrial Railway Society, 1977

Hawkins, C; Reeve, G; *An Historical Survey of Southern Sheds;* Oxford Publishing Company, 1979

Hosegood, J. G; *Great Western Railway Travelling Post Offices;* Wild Swan, 1983

Hoskins, W. G; *Devon;* David & Charles, 1972

King, S; *South West Railwayman;* Allen & Unwin, 1983

Lyons, E; *An Historical Survey of Great Western Engine Sheds 1947;* Oxford Publishing Company, 1972

Lyons, E; Mountford, E; *An Historical Survey of Great Western Engine Sheds 1837-1947;* Oxford Publishing Company, 1979

MacDermot, E. T; Clinker, C. R; Nock, O. S; *History of the Great Western Railway;* Ian Allan Ltd, 1964/67

Maggs, C. G; *The Barnstaple & Ilfracombe Railway* Oakwood Press, 1978

Maggs, C. G; *Railways to Exmouth;* Oakwood Press, 1980

Pomroy, L. W; *The Teign Valley Line;* Oxford Publishing Company, 1984

Pryer, G. A; *Exeter;* Signalling Record Society Bulletin, March 1972

Pryer, G. A; *Track Layout Diagrams of the Southern Railway and BR SR* Section 5; R. A. Cooke, 1982

Railway Correspondence & Travel Society; *Locomotives of the Great Western Railway;* RCTS 1952-74

Sambourne, R. C; *Exeter, a Century of Public Transport;* Glasney Press, n.d.

Thomas D, St J; *A Regional History of the Railways of Great Britain, Vol 1, The West Country;* David & Charles, 1981

Thomas, D. St J; *The North Devon Railway Report;* David & Charles, 1963

Tyley, F. J; *Reconstruction of St David's station, Exeter;* Great Western Railway Magazine, 1915

Vaughan, A; *A Pictorial Record of Great Western Signalling;* Oxford Publishing Company, 1973

Williams, R. A; *The London & South Western Railway,* Vols 1 & 2; David & Charles, 1968/73

Anon; *New Central Station at Exeter, Southern Railway;* Railway Magazine, August 1933

Anon; *New Distribution Depot for Messrs Cadbury at Exeter;* Great Western Railway Magazine 1930, pp 519/20

Anon; *Reconstruction of a large Railway Engineering Depot* (Exmouth Junction); Railway Engineer, February 1928

Anon; *The GWR and Electrification;* Railway Magazine, July 1939

A view showing part of the new layout at Exeter St David's. Class 50 No 50 042 *Triumph* is seen standing at Platform 1 with the 13.45 train for Waterloo. Platform 4 is occupied by the 10.45 Paddington-Penzance, 18 August 1985.   *Andrew Fox*